Eurocentrism and the Communist Movement

Robert Biel

KER
SPL
EBE
DEB
2015

Eurocentrism and the Communist Movement, by Robert Biel

ISBN: 978-1-894946-71-1

Copyright 2015 Robert Biel
This edition copyright 2015 Kersplebedeb
first printing

>Kersplebedeb Publishing and Distribution
>CP 63560
>CCCP Van Horne
>Montreal, Quebec
>Canada H3W 3H8
>email: info@kersplebedeb.com
>web: www.kersplebedeb.com
>   www.leftwingbooks.net

Copies available from AK Press: www.akpress.org

Printed in Canada

Contents

Preface ... 1

Introduction: The Significance of the Marxist Method ... 3

1. The Definition of Eurocentrism ... 12
2. The Historical Background ... 19
3. Eurocentrism and the Works of Marx and Engels ... 48
4. The Contribution of Lenin ... 103
5. The Communist Movement in the Early Twentieth Century ... 112
6. Between Lenin and Mao: The Comintern Period ... 125
7. China and the Marxist-Leninist Movement ... 148
8. Towards a Dialectical Appreciation of the Anti-Eurocentric Current of Theory ... 170
9. The Relevance of the Critique of Eurocentrism for the Twenty First Century World Order ... 191

Bibliography ... 205

About the Author ... 212
What People Are Saying ... 213

Preface

THE research on which this book is based was initially conducted in the late 1980s, and an early duplicated version was circulated widely at that time. A crucial contribution was made by discussions within the Political Economy Study Group (PESG) which was formed, under the auspices of the Revolutionary Communist League of Britain (RCLB), around this project. My major expression of gratitude is to my great friend, the late Cheikh Ahmed Gueye, for the decisive input he made into many aspects of the understanding reflected in this book.

The work responded to a strong sense that the important task was to construct a Marxist theory of political economy which could reflect the real relationships in the contemporary world system. That was the constructive task but, before we could attempt it, we also had to conduct a negative task — one of demolition: to identify and remove the blockage that stood in our way. This blockage was the thing we identified as *Eurocentrism*, a trend which imprisoned theory in an economistic and mechanical framework, denying the real dynamics of history in which the world outside the major European powers has always played such a major role, and does so still in the form of the liberation movements against all forms of oppression and neo-colonialism.

On the basis of the research conducted in the current book, I felt I was in a position to begin the constructive task, reflected in my book *The New Imperialism* (2000). In this book, I sought to show that the superficial consolidation of world capitalism (then still in a somewhat triumphalist phase) was premised on an intensification of capitalism's fundamental contradictions—on the destruction of human resources and the physical environment—and that the different forms of alienation highlighted by Marx are still fully present, and more specifically, that the global order remains profoundly racist. In my most recent book, *The Entropy of Capitalism* (2012), I have described a system now beginning to unravel under the force of these contradictions. In this sense, *Eurocentrism and the Communist Movement* forms the beginning of a trilogy, the more destructive and explicitly polemical part, aiming to clear the terrain.

★ INTRODUCTION ★

The Significance of the Marxist Method

MARXISM is essential because it exposes the fundamental facts about the destructive character of the capitalist mode of production and the need for, and possibility of, both resistance and the creation of an alternative. Although it originated in one part of the world—Europe—it provides a method applicable to situations in different countries, and will remain relevant, even to as yet undiscovered challenges, as long as the capitalist mode of production is still active. Marxism does not claim to encompass everything about the human experience, but it takes a method—dialectics—an ancient, universal principle of human thought (which itself *is* perhaps applicable to all dimensions of the human experience), and applies it to the specific question of alienation under capitalism. Alienation has a dual character: on the one hand working people are *really* alienated from the product of their own labour, which is turned into something abstract, namely capital, and becomes an instrument of tyranny over them; on the other hand, there is the illusory side of alienation—the system cloaks itself in many layers of illusion, and the task of actual struggle, guided by radical theory, is to strip these away and expose the real relations. We must therefore peel back the ideological alienation in the process of working to overthrow the real alienation through the establishment of a new mode of production.

The Marxist method is the most uncompromising critique of the ruling system because it exposes all the inconvenient realities which dominant modes of thought hide. Since the dialectical method passes continuously between the general and the particular, it can easily adapt to encompass *forms* of capitalist relations which have emerged since Marx's time, or which may arise in the future. Equally important, because it passes continuously between theory and practice, it is the repository of the immensely important experience, positive and negative, of the real movement for social change.

We could call Marxism by a more neutral name, historical materialism, i.e. the application of dialectics to the development of, and resistance to, the capitalist mode of production. In that sense, although the approach was *discovered* by Marx, we could say it had an existence independent of its origins in time and place and could well have been worked out under a different set of circumstances. Nevertheless, the reality is that it is embodied in a particular movement which originated and developed in a definite set of geographical and historical conditions. These inevitably influenced, and imposed limitations upon, the concrete form in which the theory was first put forward.

The blandest way we might state this is that there would be limitations in *any* place where the theory happened to arise (so, in political-economy-fiction, we might speculate on alternative locations and the specific characteristics or limitations these might produce). But this would be disingenuous. What concerns us are the *real* origins, and here we are getting to the crux of the matter. It is not an accident that it occurred in Europe. In the most neutral sense, we might say this happened because we are after all dealing with a theory of *capitalism*, and the nineteenth century Euro-American world was the centre of capitalist technology and ideas. This argument is not without some truth, but it would be a gross cop-out to rest content with it. Over the larger span of history, Europe's role has been marginal, both in the development of technology, and of ideas. Europe found a way of reversing this, and becoming the centre (in the sense of setting the agenda and imposing its rules, norms and culture), *through* the development of capitalism. But the way it did this was not simply by "building" itself, but by actively depleting the dynamism of the non-European world, using the latter's human and material resources, its technologies and ideas, as fuel for this building. In this way, the former hubs of human social organisation became its colonies and periphery; what was "manufactured" was not just the wonders of capitalist industry, but a phoney history in which the historicity of other societies disappeared, and European supremacy seemed natural and eternal.

The ideological fall-out of this supremacism was bound to infiltrate to some extent all ideologies evolving within the core, including those which challenge, or claim to challenge, capitalism. In the future, the Marxist movement should—and can—become truly a movement of humanity as a whole. But this cannot be conceived merely as a process of applying some pristine, correct theory to different conditions; it is also a battle to understand, and overcome, certain internal limitations of its Eurocentric origins.

This is not to say that the founders of Marxism-Leninism were passive victims of their limitations. They were capable of struggling against them, and indeed made remarkable personal progress in doing so, as we will clearly see in the cases of both Marx and Lenin. This is a measure of their greatness. But the whole point of Marxism is that the battle is won not at the level of ideas, but of social practice. It is about creating an organised movement to act within the wider context of society and its struggles. Obviously such a context would, in Europe, fall within a social system deeply imbued with chauvinism, colonialism, and racism.

Now, it is a fundamental principle of Marxism to not passively tail after the mass movement, but rather to combat its reactionary side. Most of Marx and Engels' political work was devoted precisely to this. Lenin, likewise, concentrated his energies on doing so. Then, following the Russian Revolution of 1917, the Soviet Union, owing to its status as the first socialist state, acquired enormous weight within the left. There was now a large institutional apparatus of the working-class movement which even, for a time between the two world wars, was formalised into the Third International (Comintern), a kind of global headquarters of socialism. This organised movement maintained a very strong consciousness of the need to resist the corrupting influences of imperialism. The question, however, is whether this battle was conceived correctly. If not, there was the risk that this great institutional apparatus would itself be captured by the reactionary ideas it was supposed to combat.

In the early twentieth century, a central slogan in opposing reactionary tendencies in the left was the combat against what was known as *revisionism*: the abandonment of Marx and Lenin's teachings on the inevitability of exploitation, repression, crisis, and war under capitalism. The notion of anti-revisionism will form an important part of our enquiry because it was to reassert itself strongly in the formative period of the Marxist-Leninist movement in the 1960s and '70s. It must be stated clearly that the orientation of fighting revisionism is itself correct: it will remain relevant to all periods while imperialism still exists, including today; reformists will always invent arguments to pretend that Marx and Lenin were wrong and that the capitalist system can be made calm, peaceful, and inclusive. Such arguments typically present themselves as new, up-to-date thinking based on new realities, but in substance they just re-hash the same old nonsense; it remains necessary to combat this evil.

But there are two risks in anti-revisionism. One is dogmatism: with any movement to uphold orthodoxy, you risk becoming conservative and scared of new ideas. The other is that, if the focus is miscued, that aspect of the corrupting influence of imperialism which ought to have been the target of struggle will sneak into the anti-revisionist movement and grab it from within.

This takes us to the issue of the link between revisionism and Eurocentrism. There were limitations in the original formulation of Marxism arising because of its European context, and these could only be overcome through the introduction of fresh thinking which, in the process of communism becoming a global movement, was most likely to originate from the oppressed nations themselves—only in this way could Marxism expand its horizons and become truly the movement of humanity as a whole. This kind of new thinking needed to combat Eurocentrism is qualitatively different from the pseudo-new ideas expressed in revisionism, and would in fact provide the strongest force *against* revisionism: it is precisely in the periphery, among the oppressed nations and peoples, that the true exploitative and militaristic face of capitalism and imperialism is most starkly revealed, and where reformist illusions about a peaceable and benign capitalism will be least plausible. The task of defending Marxism against revisionism is thus intrinsically linked with the task of combating Eurocentrism, and cannot be counterposed to it.

The notion of upholding an ossified "original orthodoxy" is, in any case, a contradiction in terms simply because the essence of Marxism can *only* be defended in its development: it is, and can only be, a living thing. Thus, in practice we usually find that the ossified forms of communism, particular those which gradually took over in the Soviet Union after Lenin's death, and which exercised a massive influence over the worldwide movement, were actually opposed to the original spirit of Marxism, *as well as being* hostile to the further developments which would be needed in combating Eurocentrism.

This book is intended to contribute to a historiography of a real movement, which has unfolded over decades, to combat Eurocentrism, a history which is extremely complex and tortuous, containing significant setbacks as well as remarkable lessons for the future. Given that this task cannot be realised simply in the realm of theory, we have approached it as a reflection of practice, the practice of liberation struggles and of a wide range of progressive movements. At the time when the initial research was conducted in the 1980s, the immediate context of that practice was the acute and complex struggles occurring worldwide, including those in imperialist Britain where the book was written. Pre-1980, a certain framework of social order had entrenched itself there, whereby organised labour preened itself on having acquired a recognised role in the system in exchange for promising to conduct its struggles firmly within the latter's rules. It was thus totally disarmed when Thatcher's neo-liberalism suddenly decided that, instead of co-opting organised labour (which was the previous bourgeois strategy), it was more convenient to smash it. There was a fight back, but the left's Eurocentrism made it hard to see where the forces for progress really lay: Black movements, national movements, the upsurge of the Global South and of course the superexploited sections of the British working class which had been marginalised within the labour movement just as they were in society at large. There was also a particular form of revisionism which was quite pernicious at that time: the Soviet system had, in its last gasp, been propagating a fantastically absurd theory, namely that world capitalism—stuck in an irremediable crisis and outcompeted by a dynamic Soviet bloc—would soon give up the fight and meekly hand over the reins of power ... and until this happened, exploited people should not rock the boat by struggling too hard!

The dangers of this new form of revisionism had been foreseen since the early 1960s by the Communist Party of China who, in response, initiated an extremely important historic event: a polemic to uphold the true teachings of Marx and Lenin on revolution, the state, imperialism and war. Under the impetus of this initiative, there emerged a current of more radical forces within communism in all parts of the world who were typically identified as Marxist-Leninists. A further twist occurred from the late '60s with China's "Cultural Revolution": because of the strong projection of Mao Zedong's personal role in that context, anti-revisionist Marxist-Leninists then often came to be known as "Maoists." The project that led to *Eurocentrism and the Communist Movement* was situated firmly within the context of, and under the impetus of, that historical trend.

Nevertheless, this project takes a critical, or rather self-critical, stance towards the M-L movement of which it is itself a part. The dominant Eurocentric orthodoxy on political economy, embedded in the Soviet Union, had been only partially and incompletely challenged by the Chinese. The full nature of the superexploitation of the most oppressed people remained in certain important respects weakly understood. Therefore, the scope for temporary consolidation of core capitalism on the *basis* of that superexploitation was also underestimated. The Soviets' weird and stupid theory about capitalist collapse without struggle was combated by a Chinese theory of capitalist collapse *through* struggle, which is an obvious improvement, but one which nevertheless shared with the Soviets a tendency to exaggerate the collapse of capitalism in the short term. This theory underestimated the capacity for the capitalist mode of production to adapt by co-opting some of the more amenable struggles and salvage itself by squeezing out yet more value at the expense of the oppressed nations and peoples, and of the marginalised and excluded in all countries.

Capitalism has managed to restructure itself, and regain a certain dynamism, twice: post-1945 (through Keynesianism, neo-colonialism etc.), and again post-1980 (through neo-liberalism, globalisation etc.). The first time around, the Eurocentrism of the orthodox communist movement led to a lot of confusion and denial, often because people couldn't perceive the main relationship—the exploitation of the oppressed nations and peoples—which was fuelling that restructuring. When that postwar consolidation in turn fell into structural crisis at the end of the 1960s and early '70s, it unleashed a wave of mass struggles, particularly in the South, leaving the Soviets completely clueless and in denial. The Maoists, free from the Soviet leadership's blinkered Eurocentrism with respect to the real world of struggle, correctly took up the challenge of leading the mass movement and registered extraordinary achievements which we must still affirm and learn from. But they weakly grasped the deeper relationships in political economy of which the revolutionary movement was a reflection, and too readily assumed that capitalism as a whole was irreparably damaged *at that time*, rather than merely one particular phase of it. Therefore, when once again capitalism consolidated itself (temporarily of course) after 1980, there was a fresh wave of disorientation and disempowerment, which this time affected Maoists too.

In reality, there should have been no basis for any such loss of confidence. The temporary consolidation was achieved at the expense of exporting into the (fairly near) future a more profound crisis, as we see today. By exporting exploitation more and more to the periphery, to the marginalised and disenfranchised (and, we should add, into the physical environment, an issue not addressed in this book), the system rested on increasingly weak foundations, and the fundamental contradictions described by Marx were both confirmed and intensified. But the Maoist left failed to see this relationship. Unable to understand the true foundations upon which capitalist consolidation rested, *and how weak those foundations really were*, it met the evidence of consolidation initially by denial, and then—once the evidence was overwhelming—often by capitulation. Through the 1990s, capitulationism was rife, at least in the imperialist countries.

In the case of pro-Soviet trends, this is not surprising. But surely the Maoist current, which had long seen the Soviet system as degenerate anyway, ought not to have been surprised, still less disoriented, by the collapse of a system whose bankruptcy in the face of imperialism they had long perceived? In answer to this puzzle, it seems to make sense to look for a *deep-seated* cause, and this is our contention: it goes back to the fact that colonial ideology was deeply embedded within the movement and only inadequately challenged by the critique of revisionism; it therefore lurked like a time-bomb. The danger was that the crisis of *Eurocentric* Marxism would drag Marxism as a whole down with it. We didn't wholly escape that damage, and must now seek to redress it.

As of this writing, in 2014, world capitalism is gripped by a third great structural crisis, following those of the 1930s and the

1970s. Is history repeating itself? My argument in *The Entropy of Capitalism* is *no*: the scope for a new capitalist consolidation is no longer present, and this creates a new situation. At all times, from the 1980s to the present, the objective force has existed to respond to new challenges; it exists not so much in some abstract ideal of pure Marxist correctness, but in the reality of everyday life, in actual mass struggles. These constantly expose a reality, a set of relationships of exploitation and resistance, which could be measured against the scholasticism and irrelevance of certain parts of official left-wing doctrine.

Still, we need the theory. Unfortunately, the capitulationist interlude meant that the historical continuity of the movement has been weakened. This was of course particularly the case in Europe, whereas elsewhere, notably India, the continuity still exists. Nonetheless, it remains true globally that—in contrast to the 1980s when Maoism could be traced back through an uninterrupted series of historical steps (episodes, struggles, reversals, etc.) to the movement founded by Marx—there is now a sense of hiatus, of having lost touch with those traditions. The historical sense of continuity needs to be rebuilt. The hope is that the present publication of this book will contribute to this task.

The Definition of Eurocentrism

THE communist movement has by and large not adequately assimilated the most fundamental reality of the industrial system and its society, namely racist colonial exploitation. Dialectical materialism is a correct method, but the problem is that it has not been applied universally, only selectively.

Within the left movement, important currents have always arisen to combat this weakness in varying degrees, theoretically or practically. But they often had to struggle in the margins of, and sometimes in spite of, the official movement. The anti-Eurocentric currents have therefore remained somewhat scattered. We are seeking, here, to draw them together, to define this tradition in a unified way. This is a movement to defend dialectical and historical materialism in the sense that it restores a hidden reality, and affirms the world as it really is. Insofar as Marxism is not applied in an all-round, universal way—insofar as it leaves aside the historical processes in non-European areas and the way these were distorted through exploitation by the white world—it is bound to fall prey to mechanical materialism and idealism. The departure from dialectics is thus essentially, and not just incidentally, linked with Eurocentrism, and conversely the struggle against Eurocentrism is necessarily one to develop and strengthen dialectics and to restore the historical realities upon which materialism is based.

Capitalism and imperialism are *truly* Eurocentric, in the sense that the rest of the world is superexploited by the

Euro-American world and its ruling class. This enables the ruling order not just in a narrow sense to acquire profit, but also to maintain itself *structurally*, to indulge in domestic social engineering so as to defuse the acute social contradictions which would otherwise overtake the core itself. If we pose the question in this way, it should be obvious that the main revolutionary creative forces will be found in the oppressed nations, because they are the ones on whom the system rests.

But there is also a *false* aspect to Eurocentrism. This is the ideology which presents such dominance as natural, as historically justified, as constituting the mainstream of historical progress. This ideology plays a crucial role in maintaining the unequal system, and it exists not only in society at large but within the "left" movement as well. In order to challenge the really Eurocentric world system, it is necessary to target the false ideology of Eurocentrism. We must therefore simultaneously understand both the system's reality and the ideological distortions which underpin it.

Europe used to be fairly peripheral in world history. European classical civilisation owed much to the Black civilisation of ancient Egypt, as well as to India and other areas. Subsequent European progress, including the industrial revolution, drew heavily upon achievements of these civilisations, for example the science of China and the Arab countries. Even the techniques which enabled colonial plunder, like navigation and gunpowder, came from outside of Europe. Capitalism began with an act of robbery: colonialism and the slave trade. Establishment scholars who deal in statistics just as dispassionately as their ancestors dealt in the slaves themselves spare no effort to dispute Eric Williams' thesis about the link between capitalism and the slave trade and pretend the latter wasn't a basis for accumulation. But the indisputable fact is that the development of capitalism in Europe had as its corollary the forcing-backwards of conditions in what has been sometimes called the "Third World."[1]

Indigenous industries were killed off by exports of mass-produced goods. The functioning economic systems which fed the people were forcibly replaced by cash-crops to serve the needs of industry in capitalist countries, thus creating the conditions of today's famines. The surplus value produced by the labouring population, which could have formed the basis for domestic development—albeit under a system of class exploitation—was creamed off for the benefit of further capital accumulation in the metropolitan countries. The latter maintained a tight control over the world market in order to foster a system of unequal exchange. When the exploitative international division of labour had been sufficiently consolidated, it became possible in some areas to promote a pseudo-autonomous form of "development," which is essentially subordinate and serves to accentuate factors like the dependence and dislocation of the subordinate economies, unemployment, the swelling of shanty-towns around the cities, and decadent neo-colonial culture. Such is the "civilising" mission of capitalism. Insofar as it is successful (and of course the liberation movements constitute a counter-trend which continually disputes its triumph), capitalism peripheralises the exploited areas of the world, not in relation to world history as a whole—since the active factor now becomes the liberation movements—but with respect to the dominant structures which determine and benefit from the current world economy.

Such is the reality of the Eurocentric world. On this basis there arises a distorted Eurocentric system of ideology which protects and develops along with the actual exploitative system of domination, falsifies reality and reverses it. This ideology crystallises in the form of racism. In Marxist theory, ideology is part of a superstructure placed over the "base" (the economic relations). Although this superstructure "reflects" the base, it also exercises an independent influence *upon* it. Within the false ideology of Eurocentrism, the most concentrated and acute expression is the race-doctrine, which in turn reacts upon the base to strengthen a truly racist structure of accumulation. This ideology protects the base in a number of ways, not least by infecting the left and sidetracking it from its anti-imperialist, anti-colonial tasks. Racism is thus both phoney (in its system of ideas) and very real (in its practical effects): "It is sad but salutory to realise how deeply ingrained ideas of 'race' are amongst us. In case it should be necessary, let me repeat one of my favourite paradoxes, viz. that though 'races' do not exist, racial prejudice, racialism and racism are as real as the food that you and I eat."[2]

It is vital to grasp the underlying Eurocentric ideological system as a (distorted) reflection of the world economic base of capitalism; otherwise it is impossible to understand the degeneration of those sections of the "left," and even of the anti-racist movement, which (although they may reject some of the more obvious aspects of the race-doctrine) remain imbued with a wholly chauvinist worldview wherein the *premises* of racism remain intact.

In a nutshell, this ideology imposes a false view of history which denatures the history of all societies, including the West. It is false because it is unilinear and mechanical (this again is the link between Eurocentrism and the abandonment of dialectics). The interdependence of cultures, their richness as a vocabulary of human responses to the environment, is denied. Non-European peoples are supposed to languish in barbarism or savagery, only the West is supposed to have the dynamism to attain civilisation (this is tautological since civilisation is defined in European terms!), other peoples either cannot attain this stage at all or else (according to the assimilationist line) only if they imitate and tail behind Europe, and thus accept its superiority — otherwise they are considered stagnant, possessing no intrinsic dynamic for development or historical validity in their own right, their cultures being at best only signboards along the road to what the West has already achieved. Relations amongst the great powers which squabble amongst themselves over the gains from this exploitation are considered the sole reality of world politics. Such is the Eurocentric myth.

This phenomenon was only intensified once Europe's settler-colony, the USA, assumed the mantle of world leader. The

USA is founded upon the colonial oppression and genocide of Native Americans and Blacks, as well as other nationalities. To this we can add Great Russian chauvinism, which strongly influenced the USSR during its later years of degeneration. The problem is thus in essence one of white power.[3]

THE NATURE OF "LEFT" EUROCENTRISM

Because Eurocentrism is a predominant ideology of capitalist society, it inevitably crops up also within the movements which develop as part of that society, including left movements. This does not mean that it is inevitable that the left will *succumb* to that threat, but this could be avoided only if the danger is *recognised* and therefore combated. This in turn could only be achieved by the movement adopting the standpoint of humanity as a whole and incorporating, centrally into its ideology and politics, not just the lessons of the practical revolutionary struggles of the oppressed nations but also their conceptual and theoretical perspective.

The "left" variant of Eurocentrism is essentially the same as the openly bourgeois kind, but it has certain specific features in terms of its form. Since it is the main purpose of this book to investigate "left" Eurocentrism, it is useful here to give a brief definition. It may be considered to have the following characteristics:

1) It builds upon, and in a sense takes further, the bourgeois unilinear theory of "social progress" (with Europe as the highest point, leading factor, and universal point of reference of world history). Where the bourgeoisie uses this doctrine to extol capitalism as the highest and final product of human development (the "end of history"), left Eurocentrism takes it one step further and uses this reactionary line of argument to justify also the system which is

supposed to *replace* capitalism, i.e. socialism. What follows is a corrupted definition of socialism, both in terms of its internal character and, more importantly, its international stance. In this corrupted vision, the Euro-American world inevitably continues to lead a socialist world order, just as it did the previous capitalist one.

2) It employs a false version of historical materialism to depict early capitalism as a progressive social order at a *world* level, where in reality it was only progressive, if at all, in relation to the feudal system within the major European states.

3) It underplays the role of colonialism, the slave trade, etc., as a basis for the historical origins, and ongoing accumulation, of the capitalist mode of production.

4) It schematises world history on the basis of the European experience and forces everything into this mould, as for example the expectation that all societies must have a succession of the same modes of production (slave, feudal) as in Europe, or are "backward" if they have not.

5) It holds that advanced industrial productive forces necessarily produce advanced struggles, looks down on the peasantry, conceives of revolution primarily as the sharing out of the national cake between the proletariat and bourgeois classes in the core capitalist countries (ignoring the contribution of global exploitation to the those countries' advancement, and to the production of the figurative "cake" itself), and subordinates practical political strategy and tactics to the fulfilment of this goal.

6) In its approach to international relations, it elevates inter-imperialist contradictions above the fundamental contradiction between oppressor and oppressed nations and considers relations among the great powers to be the main event in world politics.

7) It fails to see the continuing character of superexploitation and the unequal international division of labour as the fundamental basis for imperialism and seeks to explain the dynamics of crisis and restructuring in the world economy without giving pride of place to relations between the imperialist countries and the Third World.

8) It fails to recognise the extent to which the main contradictions of the capitalist mode of production have been embodied in contradictions between oppressor and oppressed nations, therefore regarding nationalism in the colonial countries as a backward, tiresome, "drag-inducing" factor; a prejudice to be treated at best with condescension.

9) It generally regards the national liberation movements as subordinate to the supposed interests of the proletarian movement in the industrialised countries, and tells them what to do.

NOTES

1. This term (which was first thought up by a European, Alfred Sauvy) has come under much criticism for being derogatory. But it did for a time play a certain role in stressing the commonalities of the struggle faced by the superexploited countries, which are mainly to be found in Asia, Africa, and Latin America.

2. Azanian People's Organisation (AZAPO) *Conference Issue* (February 1983), 29.

3. Of course we do not see world conflicts in "racial" terms, and reject the concept of "race" in its totality; but "Black" and "white" have a socio-political reality, as long as the real system of racist oppression and exploitation remains.

The Historical Background

EUROCENTRISM with its racist character is qualitatively different from whatever "ethnocentrism" may have existed in earlier periods in various regions of the world. History is full of cases where one people conquered another, but what is unique about European dominance is that Europe systematically subordinated the whole socio-economic structure of most of the world, ultimately denying the non-European world development along its own lines or even along European capitalist lines. What is special is thus the mode of production itself and its worldwide ramifications.

The racist climate of ideas developed along with (and in mutual interaction with) the actual Eurocentric exploitative system of colonialism. There are differences of opinion about how far racism was already ingrained in European society before its association with the growth of the colonial-slave system,[1] but at least the latter can be considered the key factor in its modern form.

THEORIES OF RACISM

The analysis of racism within the official communist movement, even at the time when communism was at the forefront of mass struggle, was extremely weak, apart from perhaps a tokenism which was (and still is) worse than useless. The tokenistic anti-racist perspective is always limited by the assumption that racism is "absurd": racist ideas then appear as inexplicable, haywire "dreams that have had dreams for father,"[2] lacking any objective basis whatsoever.

Of course, it is true that the entire *content* of the race-doctrine is absurd: there is no meaningful objective basis for speaking of races at all, let alone for seeing history as a battle for supremacy between them. But this does not mean the *existence* of that doctrine is in any way baffling or inexplicable. On the contrary, it came into existence for a very real reason, and that is what we have to address. Unless we face up to this, there is no way racism can be combated.

We therefore need a deep understanding of the historical context in which it arose. Although a number of interesting and important academic works have addressed aspects of the question,[3] they are generally not written from a dialectical materialist standpoint, and much of the establishment literature serves to befog the issue, an example being the tendency to equate racism with Hitlerite antisemitism,[4] neglecting the fact that Nazism can be understood only as part of a wider pattern of racism (Hitler's ideas were practically all derived from earlier anti-Black racists, many of them English).[5] The communist tradition has, shamefully, left a big vacuum where racism ought to be analysed according to the Marxist method.

Marx did, nevertheless, create what is a potentially correct basis for such an analysis. We can appreciate this if we consider his critique of Ludwig Feuerbach, a philosopher whose work played a major role in the intellectual background to the development of Marxism, but which the latter needed to transcend.

Hegel had laid a profound basis for dialectics, but Feuerbach's contribution was to overturn the idealist basis upon which Hegel's dialectics were developed; he did so by showing that ideologies are a reflection of the real world. So far so good, but as Marx then pointed out, this was not going far enough. Feuerbach cosily believed that, once you had wised up to the material realities which ideologies reflect, no one would be confused by them anymore: in place of warring religions, or any other divisions within humanity, everything would be overcome through love. That's a nice thought, but as Marx perceived, such an analysis missed the key step:

> His [Feuerbach's] work consists in the dissolution of the religious world into its secular basis. He overlooks the fact that after completing this work, the chief thing still remains to be done. For the fact that the secular foundation detaches itself from itself and establishes itself in the clouds as an independent realm, is really only to be explained by the self-cleavage and self-contradictoriness of this secular basis. The latter must itself, therefore, first be understood in its contradiction and then, by the removal of that contradiction, revolutionised in practice.[6]

This provides us with the key to defeating Eurocentrism, which is why we can say that the analysis which follows is a vindication of Marxism. But the problem is that this method was *not* applied, either by Marx himself or by the movement he inspired, to what is perhaps the most important form of alienation under the capitalist mode of production—racism.

RACE AND CLASS

On the basis of the method we have outlined, our task is to consider the real social contradictions which, plaguing the ruling order, caused the race-doctrine to develop as a response. While our main emphasis in this book will be on Eurocentrism in the left, it will be useful first to apply this approach to the wider framework within which left Eurocentrism arose. To start with, we shall consider the relationship between "race" and class.

The ruling classes have traditionally harboured a spiteful hatred of the labouring population—initially the peasantry—whom they regarded as naturally inferior, and virtually not part of the same humanity as themselves. The rigid stratification in parts of Europe in the pre-capitalist period, for example serfdom, treated the labouring class as inferior by birth. Since the nineteenth century, capitalism has learned to hide this contemptuous attitude, cultivating instead the myth of a *common* (national/racial) identity binding together rulers and ruled. However, this should not diminish our awareness of a certain tendency for the rulers to view all toilers as an inferior species, and this actually provided the basis for early race doctrines. The argument about skull shapes which played such a part in pseudo-scientific racism is partially derived from arguments put forward to justify the superiority of the aristocracy over the peasantry.[7] Reading the words of the influential nineteenth-century French racist Count Gobineau, one is above all struck by his hatred and fear of the peasantry which, he believes, "considers itself as a different species." This antagonism, he continues, would destroy European civilisation even more than any enemy from outside:

> Let us be clear about this, the base of the French population has few points in common with its surface: it is an abyss over which civilisation is suspended and the profound, immobile waters slumbering in the depths of this chasm will one day reveal themselves an irresistible force of dissolution.[8]

Later, European society was to discover that one way of defusing the domestic class confrontation was to create an artificial national unity; and it achieved this by transposing this racist dichotomy onto an enemy *outside*.

Replacing the pessimism of Gobineau, a more boisterous late nineteenth century capitalism was therefore able subsequently to build upon those ideas about the hierarchy of "races" which had originally been used to bolster feudal forms of class stratification. The ruling-class ideal of a distinct labouring class condemned to permanent subordination on genetic grounds could at last be realised, only now at a level of peoples.

Although anti-Black racism was to become the most obvious form of such national stratification, there remained a certain notion of peasant nations. We find this among the German Nazis, for example. "In the Nazi pyramid of value the peasant, excluded ideologically from the elite, represents the world where intelligence and thought in general are not of essential importance to its good functioning, nor vital for its existence."[9] The labour aristocracy in the metropolis was viewed as an embodiment of pure Aryanism, simply because it *had* managed to constitute itself as an aristocracy.[10] These Nazi ideas, unrespectable of course today within the bourgeois mainstream, nevertheless have a very "respectable" and "civilised" mainstream pedigree, which will be mentioned later. The important thing is to grasp the interrelationship between class, "race," and the national question; as we shall see, the issue of how one appraises the peasantry remains important for the analysis of Eurocentrism.

Although ideologies reflect social contradictions, a true ideology is never purely instrumental (deliberate, conspiratorial). In particular, we must be very critical of the perspective (common among British anti-racists) which views racism merely as an instrumental tactic by the ruling class to defuse class struggle. We cannot be satisfied with some image of a mythical racism being used to divert attention from a really-existing class struggle, which is moreover itself typically viewed as purely economic. A partial refutation of this error is to consider "race" as in some sense a determinant of class. Thus, "[a]ccording to the twin factors of their oppression, black people have constituted a race and a class group at the same time. The black struggle against racism, therefore simultaneously became a class struggle; the institutionalisation of inequality through legalised racism has remained a deadly class enemy of all blacks over the years."[11]

However, this response is not truly adequate. Although it is absolutely true that the class system rests upon the superexploitation of peoples of colour, who are simultaneously an essential part of the class system and excluded as pariahs within it, racism must not be *reduced* to a class issue. It is here that we must address the central role of the national question.

THE KEY SIGNIFICANCE OF THE NATIONAL QUESTION

Class is ultimately a question of status within a mode of production. Within the context of a world-scale mode of production, this inevitably has a national dimension. Early colonialism robbed subject peoples of control over their own land, and this forged the basis of an exploitative relationship which survives the transition to today's neo-colonialism.

This long process of development was punctuated by an extremely important historical watershed: the beginning of the stage called *imperialism*. Towards the end of the nineteenth century the capitalists themselves began using the term "imperialism" to boast about their conquests. We must remember that, at that time, the predominant ideology was *openly* supremacist, so they were not pretending to assimilate the "natives" and had nothing to lose by boasting about killing them. Soon afterwards the left attempted its own scientific definition of imperialism: there then followed a major debate, an understanding of which must be one of the cornerstones of our struggle for a progressive theory.

The left's imperialism debate (around the turn of the twentieth century) highlighted the fact that imperialism signifies the advent of what can be considered in some sense the "ultimate" phase in capitalism's centuries-long history: this phase, which marked capitalism's decay but which would continue for some period of time (often described as an "era"), would be populated by giant, predatory corporations and parasitic finance capital and indelibly marked by militarism and war ... but it would also somehow—through an incredibly complex and tortuous route—reveal the outlines of a new social order.

Looking at recent history as we write today (finance crisis, new wars starting all the time, oppositional social movements), the strength of that theory is obvious: we are lucky to have it, and it has stood the test of time.

Nevertheless, the rise of theories of imperialism to a central position within Marxism, important and progressive though this was, carried within it an unseen danger. The danger was to imagine that a form of capitalist development based on world accumulation from the labour and resources of the periphery only *began* with imperialism. The reality is that imperialism can only properly be understood as a development on the basis of a global, colonial-racial exploitation, ingrained within capitalism from its very origins. If we correctly view capitalism as a world system premised on colonialism, it is clear that this has always been an articulated system of production, maintaining other societies in an organically subordinate position. And this system carried with it an ideological superstructure which was similarly ingrained, which in turn was "taken over" and adapted by imperialism.

Within this superstructure, the "racial" stereotypes, far from being simply inexplicable prejudices, actually fulfil a definite role. The dependant limbo in which other societies are artificially kept becomes the germ for the notion that they are naturally "stagnant." The negative stereotypes foisted upon the oppressed are in fact a distorted projection of capitalism's *own* evils. Colonialism imposed its own violence and stirred up divisions among the oppressed peoples—the ideology depicts the oppressed as people addicted to violence who will collapse into bloodbaths and massacres if colonialism withdraws. Colonialism is an act of despotism—the ideology depicts the state system of non-European societies as one characterised by a mindless, tyrannical despotism, from which European enlightenment rescues the people. To promote the colonial act of savagery, those who oppose colonialism have to be branded "savages" and enemies of civilisation. The whole political economy is one of robbery, and within its ideology it creates for Black people the image of "muggers" or scroungers. These perspectives, dredged from the deepest recesses of the colonial psyche, survive startlingly unchanged within twenty first century discourses of "development," "conflict resolution" or "good governance"!

In this way, using the methodology of Marx's critique of Feuerbach, we can begin to understand the real basis of the race-doctrine, as well as the actual struggles through which it can be overthrown. The stereotypes are "negative" not only in the sense of being "bad"—they are negative reflections of the *reality* of colonial oppression projected onto the oppressed people themselves, with the result that the colonial and neo-colonial system appears unblemished, as a just and necessary world order. Eurocentric reality holds the world subordinated to European interests as part of a system of production. The Eurocentric myth is the turning upside down of history in order to justify this dominance as "natural." Through losing control of her/his labour, the labourer becomes alienated from her/his character as species-being (the converse of this is that the socialist revolution should be a movement for humanising society).

Of course, alienation is inflicted upon humanity as a whole, in all regions of the world including the historic core. However, it is hard to dispute that this is qualitatively more intense in the superexploited periphery. Not only do the peoples of these areas, in an economic sense, experience the vast productive forces of modern industry as an alien force opposed to their interests and exercising tyranny over them, but they also face a literal attempt to steal their humanity itself ... a necessary theft if the alien, inhuman force of capitalism is to depict itself as a humanising influence: "the Negro is more humanised when in his natural subordination to the European than under any other circumstance."[12]

For all these reasons, we cannot understand the relationship between class and "race" merely on the assumption that the "race" doctrine is a purely illusory thing, masking class realities;

on the contrary, it reflects, though in a distorted and in fact inverted form, the reality of what is the most intense form of dominance and exploitation within any mode of production.

THE RACE-MYTH — PEOPLES WITH NO HISTORY

A central element in racism is the falsification of world history. Non-European peoples were removed from history, regarded as history-less, possessing no past and no future. Eurocentrism manufactured as its historical point of reference a distorted vision of its own past: typically this hinged on a vision of ancient Greece, purged of the latter's Asiatic and African influences (so important in reality); or else a "Teutonic" past in the case of some of the Anglo-German forms of the myth. At most, in cases like China and India, some past history was grudgingly recognised, but with the proviso that this *was* all in the past: any dynamism was now exhausted, leaving these peoples stagnant and devoid of potential for *future* development. The only remaining force pushing towards the future was the European (increasingly, Euro-American) world and its economic system, capitalism.

There are three interlocking aspects to the race-myth: the struggle to control nature, the dispossession of indigenous people in areas possessing natural resources, and the struggle with rival colonial powers for the control of such areas. These concepts arose quite early in the history of capitalism. As we can see from R.H. Pearce's work, the colonial experience was a potent source for the religious ideology of nascent capitalism. By developing the resources, the colonisers were, in accordance with God's purpose, bringing order out of the chaos of these lands. In the words of Samuel Purchas, writing in 1625: "God in wisedom having enriched the Savage Countries, that those riches might be attractive for Christian suters, which there may sowe spirituals and reape temporals."[13]

This has been an abiding theme, right up to the contemporary imperialist period. What could be more characteristic of, say, the speeches of US President Eisenhower in the 1950s than the notion of a god who wisely rewards America with its riches as it nobly shoulders the task of bringing order to the world? The persistent idea is that it is legitimate, indeed mandatory, to *develop*—a notion which lies at the root of the whole concept of "development" as a seemingly philanthropic agenda—the "backward" regions which are not fit to do this for themselves. From the eighteenth century, this already provided a basis for the origins of international law:

> when the nations of Europe, which are too confined at home, come upon lands which the savages have no special need of and are making no present and continuous use of, they may lawfully take possession of them and establish colonies in them [...] if each nation had desired to appropriate to itself an extent of territory great enough for it to live merely by hunting, fishing, and gathering wild fruits, the earth would not suffice for a tenth part of the people who now inhabit it.[14]

Again, in the period of nascent British imperialism in the nineteenth century, Austen Chamberlain used to refer to the colonies as "underdeveloped estates."[15] It should be noted that the very concept of "underdevelopment," which is central to the twentieth century establishment image of the Third World's "problem," has its origins deep in the history of the capitalist-imperialist system of ideas, being used to signify areas whose resources the indigenous population **is not fit to develop, and which therefore have to be developed by someone else instead**. One finds this same order of ideas in the writings of the turn-of-the-century American geopolitical analyst Alfred T. Mahan:

> The claim of an indigenous population to retain indefinitely the control of territory depends not upon a natural

right, but upon political fitness shown in the political work of governing, administrating and developing, in such manner as to ensure the natural right of the world at large that resources shall not be left idle, but be utilised for the general good. Failure to do this justifies in principle, compulsion from outside.[16]

In the interests of being even more progressive than the bourgeoisie, certain sections of the "left" in the early imperialist period were eager to take up these ideas. Thus, according to the leading revisionist, Eduard Bernstein: "The recognition of the power which savages have over the lands they occupy cannot but be circumstantial. Basically, there too, comparatively advanced civilisations enjoy great power. What determines the historic right to use land is not their conquest but their exploitation."[17]

In this early imperialist form, the imperialists were themselves claiming the right to seize the land and take charge of "development"; in the more recent, post-World War II form, the peoples of the subject nations are told to take charge of their own "development," according to a blueprint issued from the core, in particular from its multilateral agencies like the World Bank and IMF. But the substance is the same.

THE EUROPEAN MASTER RACE

These ideas provide the framework for a fully developed race doctrine. The stereotype of Black people as scroungers ("Sitting yonder with their beautiful muzzles up to their ears in pumpkins, imbibing sweet pulps and juices"—to quote from the highly respectable establishment literary figure, Thomas Carlyle[18]) not only serves to cover up colonialist scrounging, but fulfils an even more precise ideological role. If non-Europeans enjoy the fruits of nature without having to graft for a living, they will never acquire the entrepreneurial spirit to exploit the natural resources of their countries to the full.

There are two possible deductions from this premise. In the assimilationist form, which has today become predominant, if Europeans destroy the functioning societies of the Global South, they will be doing them a favour by allowing them to become ersatz capitalists. This is the basis for today's "development" theory. But the predominant form in earlier capitalism was the exclusionist one, which considered the subject peoples simply incapable of development on genetic grounds.

Exclusionism became particularly significant once the religious form of the race-myth became threadbare, and it began to assume a pseudo-scientific garb in the form of Social Darwinism. In this form, it is supposed that Europeans have actually evolved differently: their environment has made them hardy and resourceful, inventive and creative, natural leaders. Hence they have the qualities to run not only their own countries, but the rest of the world as well. The Europeans had thus risen to a position of mastery over nature, which implied also mastery over other peoples. In the words of Eugen Dühring, a leading German racist and precursor of many of Hitler's ideas: "Now within the compass of Asiatic and especially tropical civilisations, the human being has become far more a nurseling of human nature than its master, and only the Nordic scene of his activity has matured him from economic childhood into a man."[19]

These ideas were propagated not only among ideologues but also, aggressively, within mass society in the core capitalist states. Culture played a key role in this. Thus, for example, we find the struggle-against-nature theme interlocking with the theme of mastery over foreign lands *and* their people as a central element in the novel *Robinson Crusoe* which enjoyed phenomenal popularity. O. Mannoni has conducted an analysis of the subconscious themes in this work, and although in doing so he developed his own version of a reactionary colonialist argument,[20] we can probably agree with him that *Crusoe* is an articulation of partly unconscious assumptions which tend to permeate ideology in an oppressor nation. A whole range of European popular fiction elaborated the themes of *Robinson Crusoe* and wove them into a system of ideas which acquired the status of a myth.[21] The importance of this will become clear in our subsequent argument.

Whereas early racist ideas had often been articulated in an idealist form which hid their material basis in colonialism, the subsequent pseudo-scientific stage of the race-doctrine added a further layer of complexity by creating a falsely materialist form for what were substantively the same prejudices. As a representative of the earlier, idealist approach, the great German philosopher Hegel speaks of North Africa as "a land which does nothing but follow the fate of all which arrives from the great beyond, lacking a definite face of its own. Turned like Asia Minor, towards Europe, this part of Africa could and should be attached to Europe, as incidentally, the French have recently successfully attempted to do."[22] More generally, Hegel regarded the African as representing the childhood of mankind, but at the same time, as being incapable of development *beyond* this stage, lacking in the important characteristics of Mind. Pseudo-scientific racism then came along to embody similar assumptions, but now disguised in a supposedly objective form. For example, the mid-nineteenth century writer, G. Combe in his *System of Phrenology* (New York, 1845) claimed to show objectively that the study of negro skulls revealed that "[t]he greatest deficiencies lie in Conscientiousness, Cautiousness, Ideality and Reflection."[23] This is basically just a pseudo-objective rehash of the prejudice to which Hegel had given an idealist expression, as for example where Hegel describes the African peoples as "tranquil over a long period, but they enter into ferment from one moment to another, and then become completely beside themselves" with consequences so violent because it is not an idea which has taken hold of them, but rather a "fanaticism more physical than spiritual."[24] It should be noted that these ideas reflect, among other things, the horror of the coloniser at the threat of retribution.

ASSIMILATION AND THE LIBERAL FACE OF RACISM

It is now time to consider more closely the two contradictory but intertwined aspects to the racist discourse which feed upon one another: exclusion and assimilation. Within the Eurocentric frame of reference, the non-European peoples are faced with an impossible choice. If they reject European orientations they are regarded as uncivilisable; or, if in spite of all the obstacles they attain "civilisation" according to European norms, this fact is used as evidence to prove that they can progress only with stimulus from outside. Superficially—and this has been the source of much confusion amongst would-be anti-racists—exclusionism (which condemns the subject "races" as *irremediably* inferior) seems more nasty, but in reality the two aspects are but two sides of the same coin. If you one-sidedly attack only exclusionism, you will probably end up unwittingly reinforcing racism by promoting its assimilationist form. Nineteenth-century abolitionist literature did this in a big way; it relied heavily on biographies of Blacks who had "made good," and this only became ammunition for the racists to argue that these people could at best only be imitative. Thus, in Curtin's excellent phrase, "the cultural chauvinism of the pro-Negro group rebounded to the aid of racism."[25] This remark would apply to a lot of "anti-racist" forces on the left, which have not rid themselves of a Eurocentric worldview.

Wherever the colonialist economic base needed to destroy the independent socio-economic viability of other peoples, it did so by depicting them as historically obsolete, having no future as peoples, destined to be swept aside in the course of progress. Whether this meant that they should be physically exterminated to clear the land for settler colonialism, as in parts of the Americas or Australia, or else kept in existence as a source of cheap labour, or even used in more subtle ways, for example so that the colonists could be "themselves enriched by the trafficke and commerce which may be had with them"[26] (an approach fully developed under the post-World War II regime of neo-colonialism), the argument is essentially the same. There is no massively qualitative line of demarcation between those who argued for physical extermination and those who advocated destroying a given people's identity and enslaving them. It is still a question of genocide.

Early nineteenth-century slavery debates witnessed a dispute about whether the world's peoples came from a single stock or from different stocks. The former argument is scientifically correct, because humanity comes from a single source in Africa, but at that time it was presented (by the philanthropic, anti-slavery lobbies) in a Biblical, creationist sense. Darwinism destroyed the Biblical argument, but this had the unfortunate side-effect of opening the way to a pseudo-scientific assumption that the so-called "races" were differently evolved after all. This line of argument can be found, for example, in the writings of leading British racist, Robert Knox, whose ideas anticipated, and were subsumed by, Nazism. Darwin himself rejected this deduction: his *Descent of Man* includes the statement that "there is only an artificial barrier that prevents [man's] sympathies extending to the men of all nations and races." This has often been presented as a progressive viewpoint, whereby Darwin refuted racist deductions from his theory.[27] But if we look deeper, **when it comes down to considering the realities of what was actually happening in the colonial sphere**, it is doubtful whether a qualitative difference exists between a pro-unity advocate like Darwin and an exclusionist like Knox. Darwin's conception of the unity of mankind is fully compatible with a cool, "scientific" recognition of the inevitability of the extermination of some parts of mankind by others in the interests of the survival of the fittest. As he bluntly remarks elsewhere in the same work, "where civilised nations come into contact with barbarians the struggle is short."[28] The data upon which this conclusion is based came from his actual observations of genocide. He visited Tasmania sometime after the entire native population had been deported to a barren island, where the purpose was simply to let them "die out."[29] In his journal he cheerfully remarks that, "Van

Diemen's land [Tasmania] enjoys *the great advantage* of being free from a native population. This most cruel step seems to have been quite unavoidable, as the only means of stopping a fearful succession of robberies, burnings and murders, committed by the blacks."[30]

This is a very clear expression of the chaos myth which has always been used to justify colonialism, as well as the appropriation of nature by the coloniser, taking it over from a people who were unfit to manage it. True, Darwin also condemns "the infamous conduct of some of our countrymen," but the really important point is that he regards the extinction of the weaker as an inevitable result of the clash of two social groups, however infamous the victor's means. By an obscene logic, the atrocities of colonialism are themselves used as their own justification: the fact that some peoples were exterminated proves their inferiority, according to the laws of the survival of the fittest, hence colonialism is justified.

THE "PROGRESSIVE" MISSION OF COLONIALISM — CIVILISING THE BARBARIAN

In the passage just quoted, we find another key concept of enormous significance: the notion of civilised nations versus barbarians. The concept of introducing civilisation to lands peopled by savages has been a common theme throughout the history of colonialism. The royal letters patent of 1606 for colonising Virginia state the aim, among other things, as being to "bring the Infidels and Savages living in those parts to human civility and to a settled and quiet Government."[31] (This strikingly anticipates the "good governance" theme invented more recently as an excuse for intervention!) Three centuries later, Cecil Rhodes described the Ndebele group of people (who were then offering a strong military resistance) as "the last ruthless power of barbarism that existed in South Africa" which "must pass away," arguing that "you cannot stop civilisation going into the interior."[32] As late as the 1950s, anthropologists were waging a bitter rearguard action against writers like Levi-Strauss and Michel Leiris who were accused of **undermining the distinction between the civilised man and the savage**.[33] That distinction was so important, it must be defended at all costs!

In reality, the boot is on the other foot. Insofar as barbarism and savagery have any meaning, these terms would apply to the crimes committed by colonialism in the name of civilisation. As Aimé Cesaire has pointed out, every time a head is cut off in Vietnam, or a Madagascan tortured, "civilisation acquires another dead weight, a universal regression takes place, a gangrene sets in, a poison has been distilled in the veins of Europe and, slowly but surely, the continent proceeds towards *savagery*."[34] This is precisely why it was so important for colonialism to characterise other peoples as savages or barbarians — so that its own crimes, and in fact the degeneration of its own society, might be covered up.

In the same way as phrenology was used as a pseudo-scientific gloss for prejudices about Black peoples' thought processes, so it was important in the evolution of racism in the nineteenth century for the terms barbarism and savagery to be given a supposedly scientific content, and this was to be an important task of the science of anthropology.

A key figure in this process was the American anthropologist Lewis H. Morgan. It is worth pausing briefly to consider Morgan's work, given its importance for the subsequent argument of Friedrich Engels, which we will consider in a moment.

Morgan elaborated a whole scheme of world history taking as its point of reference the development through Graeco-Roman society to contemporary capitalism. Running through this is a theme which was to play a key role in justifying genocide: the Aryan race-myth. Once again, it is highly significant that Morgan stood firmly in the "progressive" camp, in that he upheld the essential unity of humanity. Indeed the last section of his book *Ancient Society*, where he systematises his theory, is subtitled "Unity of Origin of Mankind." But, interestingly enough, he twists this in a way which, as with Darwin, *is perfectly compatible with genocide.* Summarising arguments developed earlier in his book,[35] he states,

> In strictness but two families, the Semitic and the Aryan, accomplished the work [i.e. the attainment of civilisation] through unassisted self-development. The Aryan family represents the central stream of human progress, because it produced the highest type of mankind, and because it has proved its intrinsic superiority by gradually assuming the control of the earth.[36]

In this way the new discipline of anthropology adds its weight to phrenology and other racial sciences in bolstering the "scientific" credentials of the colonialists. The key argument is, as Pearce so well expressed it, "that in the savage and his destiny there was manifest all that they had long grown away from and still had to overcome."[37] We can grasp the logic of this if we understand that, for Morgan, the thing which expresses and embodies the unity of mankind is precisely a historical continuum of which the point of reference and the culmination is the achievement of European civilisation. The act of "assuming control of the earth" by the "Aryan family" is the highest achievement of human existence, and all "savages" and "barbarians" are merely signposts on this route. But some people are still left behind at these preliminary stages, so what is to be their fate? Obviously, they either assimilate into the advanced culture ... or die! They are not really people in a living sense, but merely objects, symbols;[38] and because they do not have their own historic logic, their future exists elsewhere—it has overtaken them.

Not that the surviving savages are useless. On the contrary, according to Morgan, they can serve a useful role as material for study. Referring to the Native Americans as having been "discovered" and to their culture as "fossil remains buried in the earth," Morgan argues with some urgency that the "ethnic life of the Indian tribes is declining under the influence of American civilisation." The point for Morgan is not to *condemn* the extermination of these peoples or their cultures by American "civilisation"—indeed, it is historically necessary and laudable. But before this happens, "These circumstances appeal strongly to Americans to enter this rich field and gather its abundant harvest."[39]

In other words, by another of the obscene ironies of colonialism, the oppressed peoples, before lying down to die, are expected to submit to having their cultures dissected from an external, Eurocentric viewpoint, and thus provide evidence and building material in support of the master-race's sense of its own mission, which includes their destruction. They can thus flatter themselves with having "contributed" to building the ideological superstructure which consigns them to oblivion.

This unilinear mechanical concept of "social progress" is the essential thing which turns the "unity of mankind" argument into something objectively reactionary. It is not difficult to see how such an ethnocentric, mechanistic concept of "social progress" can crop up in a "left" guise. Having led the progress through barbarism to civilisation and on to capitalism, the Aryans can now bring the world to a yet more progressive social system, using the resources they have plundered to create an era of equality and plenty. Morgan, in his left-leaning conclusion, expresses this kind of reasoning quite explicitly, but it is at least implicitly present in very wide areas of the "left" movement.

COLONIALISM'S FEAR OF THE OPPRESSED: DEATH'S HEAD AND NO SURRENDER

A constant feature in the history of colonialism/imperialism, and hence a constant influence upon its distorted ideological superstructure, has been *resistance*. Colonial ideology always sought ways of minimising this resistance, presenting it as hopeless or using it to prove that the "natives" were essentially unruly and therefore in need of discipline.

Strategies to deal with colonial resistance have varied at different periods. At first sight we might think that the main strategic shift has moved in the direction of evolving more sophisticated, indirect, and multilateral forms of dominance. But although there is some truth in this, the sense of a unilinear development should not be exaggerated. The twenty first century now reveals extremely crude and aggressive approaches coming back into vogue. Moreover—and this is what particular concerns us here—the more seemingly "modern," indirect forms of rule arose much earlier than is often assumed. If we survey the whole history of the Eurocentric world system, informal domination rather than the possession of formal colonies appears to be a predominant feature. In many areas, formal colonisation was only a fairly brief, though important, episode in a long history of exploitation. The same point could be made about multilateralism. It is true that the dominant characteristic of the period we could call "classic imperialism" (late nineteenth century to 1945) was one of conflict between the capitalist powers in pursuit of exclusive, formal spheres of influence, economically and culturally closed off from their rivals; nevertheless, even then we find a powerful undercurrent of racist solidarity grouping all the powers together against the oppressed. In a way, this racist solidarity is what underpinned the whole edifice, so it is no surprise that such a system of multilateral oppressor-nation solidarity should establish itself so easily, in place of the earlier competitive imperialism, with the advent of the Cold War, and its successors of the "New World Order" variety. Such oppressor-solidarity is essentially based on racism; therefore, the type of chauvinism which expresses it is far deeper than the secondary form of ideology which may be expressed, for example, in cultural stereotypes about the national characteristics of rival imperialist states.

There is a potential confusion here which was to have devastating implications for the progressive camp. As we will see, the battles led by Lenin left the communist movement with a deep sense of the need to fight against chauvinism; unfortunately, however, this focused overwhelmingly on the inter-imperialist form. While in the context of World War I and its aftermath there was a certain sense to this, it carried with it a severe danger of neglecting racism. After all, in Britain immediately after that war, when the populace were pretty disenchanted with jingoism, they nevertheless launched pogroms against Black people.

Complementary to the neglect of racist exploitation is the lack of attention to struggles *against* that exploitation, the failure to recognise and declare solidarity with grassroots anti-colonial resistance: at best, such resistance tended to be seen as something primitive and atavistic which needed to be muzzled by the civilised world. This makes nonsense of the entire problematic of history. After all, the driving force for most change is struggle. The cause of progress is alive because struggle never dies down. Even reactionary changes can be understood as the ruling order's *response* to struggle, for example its evolution of indirect or co-optive means of rule, often presented under the guise of progressive support for "development."

In fact, there is a strong argument that the ruling classes often understood the reality of resistance more perceptively than the socialists. They knew it only too well, which is why they invested so much in covering it up, in some sense hoping to exorcise the spectre which resistance represented. This is clear inasmuch as, in the background of the period when race doctrines were evolving, a key issue of current affairs was the struggle of slaves in the Caribbean colony of San Domingo (Haiti), a struggle which eventually led to the formation of an independent African regime in the Western hemisphere. The struggle in Haiti became an absolute obsession with many bourgeois ideologues. As we have already noted, the race-doctrine is in many ways a product of *fear*, fear of the retribution in store for the oppressor. After the revolution in Haiti broke out, "a wave of horror and fear" engulfed American slave-owners.[40] We can now understand the duality of the response: if in some quarters there was a last-ditch defence of slavery, an alternative response was to accept the inevitability of its abolition and to *combine this with* a sharpening of the race-doctrine. **In fact, racism was all the more necessary once the abolition of formal slavery began to be seen as inevitable.** Thomas Jefferson, who made a living as manager of a slave estate before going on to draft the American Declaration of Independence, was a leading ideologue of Black inferiority. He also came to oppose slavery—out of fear. He described San Domingo as "the first chapter" and wrote: "it is high time we should foresee the bloody scenes which our children certainly and possibly ourselves (south of the Potomac) have to wade through."[41]

Leading British racist, Robert Knox[42] was similarly chilled by the spectre of the Caribbean slave revolts. Precisely because of this fear he needed to deprive the non-white "races" of their history—*in order to avoid a precedent*:

> The past history of the Negro, of the Caffre, of the Hottentot, and of the Bosjeman, is simply a blank— St. Domingo forming but an episode. Can the black races become civilised? I should say not: their future history, then, must resemble the past. The Saxon race will never tolerate them—never amalgamate—never be at peace. The hottest actual war ever carried on—the bloodiest of Napoleon's campaigns—is not equal to that now waging between our descendants in America and the dark race; it is a war of extermination—inscribed on each banner is a death's head and no surrender; one or the other must fall.[43]

Time and again Knox returns to the example of San Domingo and tries to conjure it away. The colonialist attempt to construct a Eurocentric ideology depriving the colonial peoples of a *past* was thus highly functional, with respect to the present and *future*.

Knox was only one in a long line of British racists. "Civilised" England was the source of many of the ideas which later found their "unacceptable face" in Nazi Germany. Figures from around the turn of the century who directly inspired German fascism include characters as diverse as the grand historical theorist, H.S. Chamberlain; Karl Pearson (Professor of "Eugenics" at University College, London); Cecil Rhodes, whom the German world-theorist Oswald Spengler was to glorify as the "first man of a new age"[44]; and Sir Halford Mackinder, who produced the theory of "geopolitics," a physical, geographical projection of Eurocentrism.[45] The Nazis saw dynamic Germany taking over the cause of the white races which England had served well in its time.[46] This shows, on the one hand, that there is no rigid line of demarcation between the more genteel manifestations of Eurocentrism and out-and-out racist genocide; and on the other, that there was cross-fertilisation among the European powers in terms of the evolution of racist ideas and practices. Hitler was unacceptable because, as Aimé Césaire pointed out, he did inside Europe what the other powers had long been doing outside.

COLONIAL RIVALRY: COMPETING TO EAT THE BREAD OF THE POOR

This is not to deny the importance of contradictions between the colonial powers, but these arose against a background where their collective right to rule the rest of the world is assumed. Against this background, there has occurred a transition from mercantile capital to industrial capital, from smash-and-grab robbery to the contemporary situation where this is supplemented by pseudo-independent "development" within the neo-colonial world order.

As part of this process a transitional phase occurred in the nineteenth century, involving an intense period of the expansion of formal colonialism, the effect of which was to break down the traditional structures in some areas, notably Africa—a process which, in retrospect, can be viewed as laying the groundwork for subsequent neo-colonial dependence. This objective historical logic was not necessarily consciously planned. Nevertheless, at each historical watershed, it was articulated through important policy conflicts. For example, Britain in the second half of the nineteenth century witnessed a major struggle within the political elite over whether or not it was in the national interest to expand the area under *direct* British rule. Both sides in the argument accepted the orientation of Britain exploiting the non-European world, the difference was whether this could more efficiently be done by direct rule or trade. In a wider historical time-frame we can say that exploitation through trade was to be more useful to global capitalism — that is precisely, in the more recent period, the role of globalisation and the WTO. But while the system was still moving in the direction of imperialism, the direct-rulers (for the time being) gained ascendancy. Chauvinism directed against colonial rivals developed intensively as a consequence since the expansion of one empire necessarily restricted the scope for others. But the overall premise of European dominance in one form or another was accepted by all. The greatness of the most successful colonial power was now to be demonstrated precisely by its ability to conquer the "inferior races" *more efficiently than its rivals*. As early as 1869 the leading Liberal politician, Sir Charles Dilke, wrote in his book *Greater Britain*, "China, Japan, Africa and South America must soon fall to the all-conquering Anglo-Saxon. Italy, Spain, France, Russia become pygmies by the side of such a people."[47]

The race-doctrine was thus adapted to these new needs, and soon Karl Pearson was to formulate these concepts "scientifically" in his book *National Life from the Standpoint of Science*: "A nation ... is an organised whole ... kept up to a high pitch of external efficiency by contest, chiefly by way of war with inferior races, and with equal races by the struggle for trade-routes and for the sources of raw materials and of food supply."[48]

The trend of chauvinism between the great powers was a newly developing factor in the period leading up to the thirty years of acute crisis and war experienced by the imperialist system in the period 1914–45. As we know, the workers' movement faced a grave challenge during this period: the capitalists of each country were encouraging workers to align with their "own" bourgeoisie on patriotic grounds, which threatened to divide the movement, fostering collaboration and class capitulation. This danger was highlighted and a great struggle unleashed against it, notably under the leadership of Lenin. This struggle was definitely correct in its own terms; it pinpointed the fact that the bourgeoisie of all countries were, in the last analysis, united as exploiters, or as Brecht rightly put it, "[b]ut now, united round the table, they are eating the bread of the poor."[49] However, the more basic question of the racist chauvinism underlying the Eurocentric system was not brought to the fore in this struggle. The bourgeoisie were united not just as class exploiters, but as the white world against the Global South—whose bread, in the most fundamental sense, they were eating. It would be extremely dangerous if the workers' movement were to fight the battle against class collaboration only to fall prey to this more fundamental collaboration; indeed, were they not to question "race" solidarity, there is no way they *could* actually avoid class capitulation.

NOTES

1. The case for the lack of racism in the ancient white world is strongly argued in F.M. Snowden's *Before Colour Prejudice* (1983), although the author makes some fundamental flaws in his analysis of ancient Egypt. The case for racism's long history in European society is developed by C.J. Robinson in *Black Marxism* (1983): these arguments need to be studied very carefully, although Robinson seems to bend over backwards to devalue the concept of class struggle. Shakespeare's *Othello* is sometimes cited as an example of a non-stereotyped view of

a Black man, but Peter Fryer, in *Staying Power* (1984), demonstrates that this work was exceptionally non-pejorative by the standards of the time. (Fryer, 140) Also, Othello is still a character embodying uncontrolled passion.

2. Yeats, 500.

3. R.H. Pearce's *The Savages of America* (1965), W.D. Jordan's *White over Black* (1968), and P.D. Curtin's *The Image of Africa* (1965), are all examples of really interesting books which need to be read.

4. An example of this trend is G.L. Mosses' *Toward the Final Solution* (1978).

5. It is worth noting that even on German Nazism the serious analytical literature is quite weak, which reflects American efforts to make sure nothing distracted from anti-communism during the Cold War period. See, for example, Nolte's "The Problem of Fascism in Recent Scholarship" in the collection *Re-appraisals of Fascism* (1975).

6. Marx and Engels, *Selected Works*, Volume I, 14.

7. This concept was still put forward even at a fairly developed stage of the Aryan race-myth, for example in the work of Georges Vacher de Lapouge (Nolte, *Three Faces of Fascism*, 358).

8. Gobineau, 101–102, author's translation.

9. N'Dumbe III, 165.

10. Nolte, *Three Faces*, 635 § 18.

11. Abraham, 22.

12. Quoted in Taharka, 31. From James Hunt's (President of the Anthropological Society of London) "On the Negro's Place in Nature" (1864).

13. Quoted in Pearce, 8.

14. Curtin, *Imperialism*, 45. Quoting Emer de Vattel's *The Law of Nations* (1758).

15. Field, 89.

16. Quoted in Leith, 21. From Mahan's *The Problem of Asia* (1900).

17. Quoted in *L'Impérialisme Aujourd'hui: Traité sur l'Impérialisme, Stade suprême du capitalisme,* 238. From Bernstein's "The Premises of Socialism and the Tasks of the Socialist Party."

18. Quoted in Curtin, *Imperialism*, 138. From T. Carlyle's "Occasional Discourse on the Nigger question" (1849).

19. Dühring, 74–45. Author's translation from the original German.

20. See Mannoni's *Prospero and Caliban* (1956). Although it was first published in French in 1950, the English edition has an extremely reactionary preface by the Director of Studies in Race Relations at the Royal Institute of International Affairs, which makes it even better negative material. A forceful critique of Mannoni is made in Cesaire's *Discourse on Colonialism*, (1972).

21. See Ridley's *Images of Imperial Rule* (1983). This is a very interesting book, but unfortunately the author swallows Mannoni uncritically.

22. Hegel, G.W.F. *La raison dans l'histoire* (Paris: 10/18). Author's translation.

23. Quoted in Curtin, *The Image of Africa*, 367.

24. Hegel, op. cit., 266.

25. Curtin, *The Image of Africa*, 386.

26. Pearce, 19. Quoting an argument put forward in Maryland in 1635.

27. *October* I:2 (1980s), 9.

28. Curtin, *Imperialism*, 45. Quoting from Charles Darwin's *The Descent of Man*.

29. The system believed it had succeeded in this although today the descendants of these indigenous populations are vigorously asserting their continued existence.

30. Darwin, 430. Author's emphasis.

31. Pearce, 6.

32. Vindex, 343–344. From a speech by Rhodes in Bulawayo in 1893.

33. Cesaire, 45.

34. Ibid., 13

35. Morgan, 39.

36. Ibid., 562

37. Pearce, ix.

38. Fei Xiatong's *Towards a People's Anthropology* (1981) makes some very good points in arguing that a progressive anthropology must be people-based: "It seems that these living people [the indigenous population of the Trobriand Islands in Melanesia] were long gone from the minds of our anthropologists and what they knew and what they kept talking about was the mere shadow of these people dancing under my tutor's [Bronislaw Malinowski's] pen nib." While this is an excellent critique of Malinowski, Fei shies away from a direct confrontation with Morgan. This is presumably because of the association between Morgan and Engels, which we will examine below.

39. Morgan, vii–viii.

40. Du Bois, 71.

41. Quoted in Jordan, 434.

42. A former surgeon, Knox served with the British Army in Azania (South Africa), and thus had an opportunity to witness the freedom struggle first hand. Returning to the British Isles, Knox became implicated in one of the most notorious of the chilling crimes which so obsessed Victorian England: the Burke and Hare bodysnatching case. Deprived, as a result, of his right to practice medicine, he became a professional racist. His racist lectures are written in a very popular and demagogic style. No one in the socialist movement took people like him seriously.

43. Knox, 244–245.

44. Spengler, 37. Spengler was criticized by the Nazis for his pessimistic worldview, but not on this question.

45. For the Nazis' admiration of Mackinder, see Hayes, 26; Maser, 122.

46. See Schneefuss, 121.

47. Quoted in Huttenback, 16.

48. Quoted in Hayes, 24.

49. Bertolt Brecht's *Die Dreigroschenoper* (author's translation).

Eurocentrism and the Works of Marx and Engels

THE fundamental relevance of Marxism lies in its potential to uncover the realities of exploitation—it exposes the realities which other ideologies cover up through false promises to promote generalised wealth. Today this is more relevant than ever: the globalisation discourse tells us to worship something called "growth," which allegedly creates plenty, and is hence the basis of wider distribution and general welfare. But what capitalist economists call growth Marxism calls accumulation. Accumulation means not just the expanded reproduction of capital, but also its concentration in a few hands. Poverty is therefore inevitably manufactured as a byproduct of wealth-creation. The ruling order has every interest in preventing the working masses wising up to these realities. As the *Communist Manifesto* rightly says: "[t]he proletariat, the lowest stratum of our present society, cannot stir, cannot raise itself up, without the whole superincumbent strata of official society being sprung into the air … What the bourgeoisie therefore produces, above all, are its own grave-diggers."[1] To interpret this vision creatively, it must be understood at a global level. The lowest stratum of present global society is undoubtedly the marginalised, the superexploited, the peoples of colour, the working masses of the South and those forced to migrate. That quote from the *Communist Manifesto* is fully applicable to today's reality, we simply have to make the unit of analysis the whole of humanity; there are no fundamental reasons why Marxism cannot be creatively developed in this way. Tremendous achievements along these lines were, for example, made by the dependency theories of the 1970s. Samir Amin, in particular, correctly pointed out that the truth of Marx's thesis about pauperisation (the manufacture of poverty as a byproduct of accumulation) is revealed in all its intensity only if one takes the North-South dimension into account.

This transition is perfectly natural and logical, but this does not mean that, historically, it was straightforward or easy to realise. Marxism had to shake off the limitations of its origins within that region which *dominated* the world system, and whose culture reflected that domination. Europe claimed a right to world leadership in terms not just of economics, but in the development of ideas, and the immediate origins of Marxism occurred within this framework. Lenin is quite right in identifying the three sources of Marxism as German philosophy, English political economy, and French socialism. But the mistake which Lenin made—though as we will see in detail later, he was able to a significant extent to overcome this error in his subsequent work—was to equate this European intellectual heritage with "the highroad of development of world civilisation."[2] On the contrary, this origin carries with it a *limitation* which needs to be overcome so that the universalism of Marx's doctrine can be realised.

Marx provided a general framework within which such limitations *can* be overcome. This is because of his mastery of dialectics, a method which helps us understand how each phase of apparent progress under capitalism only gives way to a different form of regression; and revolutionary ideologies must understand *this whole process*, and their own historical place within it.

For example, the eighteenth-century Enlightenment dismantled the obscurantist systems of feudalism, where religious ideas were manipulated to bolster class oppression, but only to replace this with mechanical materialism—a unilinear doctrine of progress which itself bolstered the rule of the bourgeoisie. As a weapon against mechanical materialism, Marx employed a remarkable discovery which he inherited from his predecessors in the German tradition, Hegel and Feuerbach, and himself developed in a brilliant way: dialectics. It shows that the reality of a thing is the contradiction within it, that development proceeds through the negation of the negation. The identity of each new stage in a process is determined by what it is *not*, by what it demarcates itself from, i.e. the characteristic of the stage which it has just negated. The act of destruction therefore implies the persistence of the thing it has destroyed, which is carried forward in a "suspended" negative sense, until the next phase-transition arrives to reverse that negation, enabling the earlier characteristic to re-emerge in a changed form. This is precisely why the progressive developments of capitalism, in negating feudalism, may carry within them far more comprehensive forms of material exploitation and ideological alienation. This is obviously also a danger which *could* arise within socialism, if we view it merely as a unilinear progression from capitalism, and indeed the potential for a critique of the degeneration of socialism along these lines could be an illustration of the immense critical power of dialectics when applied to new problems.

Now, it is our contention that the most fundamental form of mechanical materialism is not the bourgeois doctrine of social progress but Eurocentrism. There is absolutely no doubt that Marxist dialectics can be applied to analysing and resolving this problem, as we are attempting to demonstrate in this book. But in the concrete form in which dialectics arose at this time, it was *itself* somewhat infected with Eurocentrism and partially harboured within it the thing which it ought to criticise. As a natural system of human thought, dialectics was present in many ancient belief systems throughout the world, in varying degrees overlaid or distorted by exploiter-class ideologies. The form in which Hegel discovered it was that expressed by the ancient Greek pre-Socratic philosophers, who themselves had derived it from Asia. But Eurocentrism wrongly depicts classical Greece as something inherently European instead of as (in reality) a conduit to the non-European world. While it was the intuitive brilliance of Marx to enshrine dialectics at the core of his thinking—and this is precisely why Marxism will always retain its relevance—the *heritage* of dialectics was not well understood. Hegelian dialectics negated mechanical materialism, but only imperfectly. There are distortions in Hegel's concrete application of his own method, as we have already noted in regards to the question of Africa. While dialectical materialism is a correct theory, its potential can therefore only be realised if we draw together the contributions of the systems of thought of different human societies.

It is itself an important expression of the historical dialectic that the basic revolutionary forces of the world oppressed by capitalism should themselves take hold of Marxism, explicitly or implicitly criticise its shortcomings, and universalise it, making it a treasure for the whole of humanity. This has indeed occurred within the mass movement and among important thinkers and leaders who have emerged from the oppressed nations. But the problem is that this development has taken place to a large extent—particularly after Lenin's death—*in spite of* the official communist movement rather than because of it. That movement has at best ignored and at worst set itself against such a development. It is true that, from an ideological point of view, the degenerations which have occurred within the history of communism have happened through a process which was to a significant extent one of degeneration *away from* the correct ideas of Marx and Engels; nevertheless, some of the errors also involved an important element of magnifying certain initial weaknesses which existed within the principles of communism as formulated by them, weaknesses which arose where the Eurocentric limitations of these leaders made them depart from a consistent application of their own dialectical and historical materialist method.

Although, as we will see in a moment, Marx and Lenin continued throughout their lives to develop this method, and were able to make progress in overcoming some of the influences of Eurocentrism within their thinking, it will be important first to consider what some of the key limitations, expressed in the founding works of Marxism, really were.

FACTS AND THE RE-EXAMINATION OF HISTORY

The actual and potential trend to develop Marxism in a non-Eurocentric direction is not something which can occur in an isolated way within the realm of theory. It is above all a product of practice. Insofar as radical theory attains a position where it can highlight the real historical processes involving humanity as a whole, this can occur only because the oppressed nations have in reality, in struggle, pushed themselves onto the stage of history. The creativity of the national liberation movements has opened up conditions for exposing the Eurocentric myth in the present while also forging links with the past historical creativity and identity of non-European peoples. The actual struggle poses the necessity of probing, through revolutionary theory, the contradictions which lie at the basis of that struggle.

We can take as our starting point a beautiful formulation from the work of Engels. Speaking of the working-class uprisings in Lyon, France in 1831, Engels argued that they not only gave the lie to the theories of the identity of interest between capital and labour, but also at the same time gave an impetus to the movement for change in the field of the science of political economy. As he put it: "The new facts made imperative a new examination of all past history."[3] This can be our watchword in the enquiry which follows.

On a much larger scale, we can say today that the national liberation movements have made necessary a re-examination of the whole history before and since the origins of capitalism, as well as the history of the movement *against* capitalism. Actually, these "facts" are not really "new": struggle always existed as the complementary opposite of colonialism itself, but the perception of it is certainly new. The two key ideas to emerge out of such a re-examination are, firstly, a systematic conception of colonialism and slavery as the essential elements in the growth of capitalism and, secondly, the historicity of non-European societies, which was interrupted through colonialism but which reasserts itself through the anti-colonial movement. These ideas are not just a development of left theory, but also a subversion of ruling class ideology, i.e. Eurocentrism, which supports the colonial system. In general, any development of revolutionary theory also attacks the ideological supports of the established order.

But this process of the expansion of revolutionary ideology to encompass the whole of humanity certainly does not proceed smoothly because it encounters Eurocentrism not only externally, but internally. The nineteenth century, the formative period of socialist thought, was also a period of expansion and consolidation of the colonial system, and a systematisation of its ideology, particularly in the form of the race-doctrine. There was a real struggle between European and non-European societies (one between colonialism and resistance), which the racists theorised into a false doctrine, i.e. a Social Darwinist struggle between so-called "races." It cannot be said that the historical process of the emergence of the race-doctrine, or the distorted interpretation of history to which it gave rise, received a serious challenge from the left, *or even a serious recognition that it existed*. The function of socialist thought should have been to drag into the open issues which the bourgeoisie suppressed, ask the awkward questions (ones which socialists successfully asked in the domestic sphere, for example, "who produces the wealth?"), to show that what was really happening was not a struggle between "races," but rather capitalism's superexploitation according to colour. On this basis, a truly world-encompassing understanding of capitalism could have been attained, instead of the inevitably truncated view which could result if one were to concentrate exclusively on the analysis of processes *within* a metropolitan country. But because socialism failed to meet this challenge, *and in fact more or less ignored it*, the dominant system was able to retain a monopoly of the *interpretation* of the really-existing conflicts between oppressor and oppressed nations, which they used to promote the race-doctrine.

MARX AND MALTHUS

Marx failed to give effective leadership in meeting this challenge. In fact, surveying his body of work, one would hardly have the impression that it was contemporaneous with one of the most influential and pernicious developments in the history of ideology—the elaboration of the race-doctrine.

Among all the ideologues whose ideas were to be incorporated into the race-doctrine, there was only a single one to whom Marx paid significant attention. This was the earlier writer Thomas Malthus, whose ideas about the competitive pressure of population upon scarce food resources predated the elaboration of "scientific" forms of racism, but were subsequently pressed into service to provide an important support for the survival-of-the-fittest, Social Darwinist line of reasoning. Marx's attacks on Malthus were therefore significant. But their theoretical basis was nevertheless quite confused. This will supply a useful point of departure for our argument.

Marx criticised Malthus on the grounds that his view was ahistorical: "Malthusian man, abstractly deduced from determinate man, exists only in Malthus's head."[4] But this criticism in itself is by no means a step forward. In order to see why, we have to look at the relationship between Malthus and capitalism. The system needed Malthus because his argument that history is determined by population growth was a convenient way of distracting attention away from class struggle (neo-Malthusian arguments keep popping up even now, with a similar purpose). This is precisely why Marx wanted to attack the theory, and within these limitations he was right to do so. However, the co-opting of Malthus into the service of capitalism was not without its own problems. Nostalgic for a stagnant vision of social order, his worldview is essentially static and pessimistic; he does not believe in a bright new future under *any* social system, even capitalism. Since for him all societies are static, there are no reasons for regarding non-European ones as inferior. From this standpoint, Malthus has no particular interest in arguing for a civilising or progressive mission for Europe. He thus argued *against* colonisation; despite the ignorance of his writings on Africa he recognises the existence of "negro *nations*,"[5] and in connection with Mexico and Peru he even writes: "We cannot read the accounts of these countries without feeling strongly that the race destroyed was, in moral worth as well as in numbers, superior to the race of their destroyers."[6]

As a staunch conservative, Malthus opposed the ideas of progress put forward in the eighteenth century enlightenment. However the latter, insofar as its conception of progress was mechanical rather than dialectical, actually held within it the seeds of a vulgar evolutionism which could easily be pushed in the direction of pseudo-scientific forms of racism (as we already saw in the work of Morgan, for example). Simply to introduce historically determinate man in place of Malthusian man could open the way to the "historical determination" of other societies as "primitive" in contrast to progressive Europe. One cannot therefore say that Marx's lines of demarcation with Malthus were correctly drawn.

In furthering our understanding of the progressive potential—and practical limitations—of Marx's position, let's consider more closely the question of "historically determinate man." Another key figure whom Marx criticised for talking about an abstract individual rather than an active, practical, social being, was Ludwig Feuerbach. In itself, Marx's critique was an important achievement, and the passage we have already quoted from his *Theses on Feuerbach* provides a sound basis for a historical materialist critique of Eurocentrism: Feuerbach correctly saw that ideologies reflect the alienation of the human from her/his essence as species-being, but, whereas Feuerbach thought this alienation could be overcome at the level of consciousness,[7] for Marx alienation in the realm of consciousness is only a reflection of self-contradiction in the secular basis (the material world), and this must be resolved through revolutionary practice.

But Marx's line of argument, though correct in principle, contains a hidden trap-door through which Eurocentrism could enter. Feuerbach's abstraction and lack of historical specificity leads him to relate to the whole of humanity as a species, and to reject divisions. Thus he affirms: "[i]t is only since the power of faith has been supplanted by the power of natural unity of mankind, the power of reason, of humanity, that truth has been seen in polytheism, in idolatry generally."[8] This point of view is on the one hand extremely progressive, yet on the other insufficient. The progressive aspect is that it can lead us towards a perception that all peoples of the world have their own historical validity and, through their cultures, express different facets of a common human striving to come to terms with the natural world in the course of production and life in general, facets of a mutually enriching human endeavour. At the same time, there are valid criticisms which can be made, but perhaps not the ones which Marx and Engels did make. Engels—in his book *Ludwig Feuerbach and the End of Classical German Philosophy*—simply refuted the above argument by Feuerbach by saying that people think differently according to class.[9] This is a really weak riposte. In the spirit of Marx's theory of alienation we can outline a stronger critique. It is pointless merely, as a sentimental pious wish, to affirm the unity of the human race unless we also recognise the *actual* history and present experience of racist oppression—which underlies the ideology of racism—and take steps to resolve this material cleavage of society in practice. This position, which follows logically from Marx's premises, subsequently found expression in sections of the Black liberation movement, for example the Black Consciousness Movement of Azania (South Africa).

But Eurocentrism prevented Marx himself from following his premises to this logical conclusion. If one tries to overcome Feuerbach's abstractness by bringing into play a conception of concrete, historically-determinate "reality" which is narrowly Eurocentric, it is perfectly possible to arrive at conclusions *which are worse than Feuerbach's*. Thus Marx could describe the Hindu religion as "a brutalising worship of nature, exhibiting its degradation in the fact that man, the sovereign of nature, fell down on his knees in adoration of Hanuman, the monkey, and Sabbala the cow."[10] This is surely a step backwards from Feuerbach's affirmation of respect for traditional belief systems.

It is our argument that the highest form of alienation of mankind from our basic humanity is that created by colonialism, the slave trade and imperialism, and the racist Eurocentric ideology with which these interact. This is the main issue in the capitalist era rather than religious alienation. Naturally, oppressed people will assert their resistance by affirming their historic culture, of which an important component is their belief-systems; if religious movements sometimes take fundamentalist forms, this is to a significant extent because the left has failed to come to grips with alienation in a comprehensive way. Perhaps Marx's failure to do justice to his brilliant concept of alienation in his later works can be ascribed to his inability to understand the direction in which it *needed* to be developed, to understand humanity and the reality of oppression in a broad enough way. Unless the real divisions engendered by colonisation are taken seriously, and struggled against in practice, there is no possibility of building a revolutionary unity among all working people. Racism could even be strengthened if you were to stop short at saying that people think differently in different modes of production.

MARX ON COLONIALISM[11]

This takes us to one of the most important issues within Marxist theory: the question of the correct attitude to take in regards to the break-up of traditional systems by capitalism. Capitalist society began with an *internal* act of the overthrow of tradition, an act of plunder and violence within its own frontiers: the enclosure of common lands in England, for example, ended the rural subsistence economy and left working people destitute, forcing them to accept the most appalling conditions in nascent industries. But it also, more or less at the same time, did something similar internationally, through colonialism and the slave trade: these were not simply acts of *exploitation* but, more fundamentally, put an end to whole modes of production. The plunder and violence in the international form of destruction were even worse than in the domestic.

How are we to assess these processes historically? The violence and atrocities of these *origins* was indeed recognised in Marx's work: in *Capital*, he described capital coming onto the historical stage dripping with blood from the slave trade, the colonisation of India, etc. But on its own, this recognition is insufficient for three general reasons. First of all, the material contribution of such destruction to capitalism itself is here considered essentially "primitive": primitive accumulation is the *initial* injection of value which supposedly enables subsequent circuits of accumulation to be self-sustaining. This leads directly to the second weakness: we might, in the above argument, think that capitalism has somehow developed or progressed *beyond* its bloody past, becoming more urbane and civilised. Such an assumption would be nonsense in terms of the reality we see around us today: capitalism doesn't just *enter* the stage of history dripping in blood from international plunder, it needs to be drenched in fresh blood all the time. Thirdly, and this is the most problematic aspect of all, Marx's formulation could be consistent with seeing the destruction as somehow progressive: although conducted in a bloody way and from the basest motives, it might still have been historically "necessary," for example in removing the stagnancy, narrowness, and fragmentation of traditional village life; this latter is the bourgeois modernist perspective, and we have to think carefully about where it may have crept into Marx's thinking.

The linear approach would say that old socio-economic systems should be, or at least inevitably will be, swept away, making room for capitalism, which would eventually in turn give way to socialism. We must seriously understand how wrong this approach really is. If anything, the experience of the twenty first century suggests that the further capitalism develops, the *more* bloody it becomes. It is true that today's system falls within the era of imperialism, a degenerate form of capitalism, as expressed in its military-political superstructure and parasitism; nevertheless, it would be nonsense to say, "in the beginning we have a bloody primitive form and at the end a bloody decadent form," because that would neglect precisely the thing which links these two together into a single continuum: the act of accumulation itself. To re-emphasise, we must not think of an initial, primitive injection from the act of destruction launching circuits which are subsequently self-sustaining. One of the most remarkable contributions in critiquing this notion was made around the beginning of the twentieth century by the great revolutionary Rosa Luxemburg, whose ideas were misunderstood and marginalised within the subsequent official communist movement. She considered the breakup of traditional systems as intrinsic to the continuing process of capital accumulation: "overseas, it [capital] begins with the subjugation and destruction of traditional communities, the world historical act of the birth of capital, since then the constant epiphenomenon of accumulation."[12] The extraordinary commodification of everything in the post-1980 form of global capitalism (structural adjustment, privatisation, the commodification of every aspect of culture and leisure and even of life itself) surely confirms this prediction. Luxemburg's contribution is an example of how a creative application of the Marxist dialectical method can yield powerful analytical tools.

Of course, linear thinking is incompatible with Marx's method but, in combating it, Marx himself had at least one hand tied behind his back. He rebelled against the limitations, but incompletely; this is the process we must now trace.

Before we consider the approach to populous traditional societies, it will be very interesting to explore a still more fundamental concept in bourgeois colonial thought, the image of so-called "virgin land," land which was supposedly unoccupied. In reality, humanity being so adaptable, populations and cultures existed virtually everywhere in the pre-colonial period; so the virgin lands idea was, besides its sexist and macho implications, a total myth, but a convenient one. Marx fell into this trap more than once. In fact, in the case of settler colonies where the colonialists wanted to wipe the indigenous people off the map and replace them, Marx was prepared to write them out of history at the stroke of a pen. In the address to Abraham Lincoln which he wrote on behalf of the International Working Men's Association during the American Civil War, Marx in no way questions the right of white settler colonists to exploit the "virgin soil" of America—he simply objects to the use of slave labour in so doing.[13] Moreover, it is extremely interesting that *Capital* Volume I, which is in a way the lynchpin of the whole of Marx's work, actually concludes with a discussion of colonisation: but one which is conducted in a very strange and distorted way. Marx addresses the issue entirely at a level of contradictions between the metropolitan bourgeoisie on the one hand, and European settlers on the other. And in this passage, Marx again returns to the "virgin soil" theme, stipulating that "[i]t is a question of true colonies, of a virgin soil colonised by free emigrants."[14]

This position virtually aligns itself with a key colonial myth, one which generated, for example, the Afrikaaner notion that southern Africa was empty when colonists arrived. There were in reality practically no instances of colonisation which did not involve the dispossession of a people who had made that particular portion of the natural world their own, nurturing it through a society and culture which developed in harmony with its characteristics; and if it is true that in some areas the population was sparse, this only reflects the fact that populations, by their very existence in harsh conditions, had provided valuable experience for humanity in the sustainable management of marginal lands. In the post-capitalist era, and in that of the anti-imperialist movement which precedes it, the world's people will need to be conscious of the environment and draw on the whole of this vocabulary, the range of responses which have been hitherto evolved.

The above argument is interesting because it addresses some of the most profound elements of colonial thinking, upon which the whole of the edifice is constructed. Bearing this basis in mind, let's now consider the issue of territories which could not be considered "virgin," i.e. those where there was already a civilisation long before colonialism—like India.

In cases like this, Marx had a strong tendency to view the destruction of their traditional economy as something progressive. This comes across clearly, for example, in his piece "The British Rule in India." While Marx and Engels constantly condemned the atrocities of colonialism, at the same time they took pride in proving they were not soppy liberals, by hard-headedly praising the centralisation of the market which was *objectively* brought about by these regrettable means. Thus Marx writes:

> I have continued this hidden warfare in a first article on India [i.e. "The British Rule in India"], in which the destruction of the native industry by England is described as revolutionary. This will be very shocking to them. As for the rest, the whole rule of Britain in India was swinish, and is to this day.[15]

Now in fact, notions of the backwardness, isolation, and stagnancy of Indian traditional production were just as much a myth as that of the Americas being "virgin" land. They are nothing more than an aspect of the *ideology* which reflects the needs of European industry. Thus a bourgeois economist, Henry Fawcett, who was known as a "friend" of the Indians and, like Marx, vigorously condemned the atrocious *methods* of colonisation, nevertheless argued that the break-up of communities was indispensible for the development of cash-crop production—which was of course in India's best interests!

> A village community virtually isolated from the rest of India cannot now raise that produce for which their land is best adapted, but must cultivate it with a view of supplying themselves with the first necessities of life. Manchester would, no doubt, annually purchase off India many million pounds' worth of cotton.[16]

Here the link with economic interests is fairly transparent, but this ideological position gave rise to a whole way of seeing the Indian situation. Marx largely remained a prisoner of this dominant ideology of his time, and this fact stood in contradiction to the logical development of historical materialism.

In the case of Ireland, in contrast, Marx and Engels were able to make a theoretical breakthrough in understanding the fact that the colonial imposition of capitalism is not in any sense a step forward, quite the contrary: "Ireland has been stunted in her development by the English invasion and thrown centuries back."[17] This is an extremely important statement, which supplies a template which could be applied to the colonial situation in general. But this is just what Marx himself mostly didn't do.

"STAGES" THEORY OF HISTORY

The unilinear bourgeois view of history sees "advanced" capitalist society as the summation of everything worth preserving in earlier phases of development, and at the same time a vantage point from which they can be appraised—as for example in the "stages theory" of the avowed apologist for US imperialism,

W.W. Rostow.[18] Around the declining phase of the Soviet order, one East European writer gave an excellent critique of Rostow, which in fact has a much wider applicability. He critically characterises the "stages" model thus:

> If a society classified amongst the highest group has certain characteristic features, then every society that reaches this stage owing to the development of its productive forces, will assume the same features. Moreover, in order to reach this stage, on the strength of its productive forces, it must develop these very characteristics.[19]

The irony is that this critique would apply just as much to the then-prevalent Soviet view as it would to the American: the Soviets, too, viewed their so-called socialist society as the point of reference for every pre-existing phase. So by what process did the Soviet Union come to develop a view so close to that of capitalism? To begin with, it is very important to state that the Marxist concept of modes of production is in principle *not* the same as the bourgeois doctrine of progress and modernisation. For example, in its true dialectical form, Marxism recognises (as we will see in a moment) that (advanced) socialism can build itself directly on certain aspects of traditional social networks, without the latter having first to be destroyed by capitalism. But without doubt, the concept of modes of production has shown itself *open to the risk* of being infiltrated by the dominant, linear, and deterministic views characteristic of capitalism's perspective on progress. As early as the 1920s and 1930s, Soviet theory had developed a very questionable model of a rigid succession of modes of production (primitive communism, slavery, feudalism, capitalism, socialism) which is not only dogmatic in comparison with Marx's own view, but also imposes a Eurocentric straitjacket on other societies (for example, feudalism was very characteristic of Europe but its features are not necessarily reproduced elsewhere).

If capitalism claimed to be a superior vantage point from

which to judge all previous forms of society, then any definition of socialism built upon a Eurocentric, unilinear notion of development could be expected logically to make a similar claim. Such a perspective is wholly foreign to historical materialism; it finds, nevertheless, a certain basis in some of Marx's writings when he himself departed from the correct premises of his own philosophy. An example is the following:

> The categories which express the relations of this [bourgeois, i.e. European] society and make possible the understanding of its structures permit us at the same time to grasp the structure and production relations of all past societies, on the ruins and with the elements of which it built itself up.[20]

This is too simplistic. In reality, global capitalism has not incorporated within its structures the things which it destroys in traditional societies: the essential strivings of humanity for self-realisation, the spiritual dimension, the unity with nature. Those things are still *present* within the characteristics of the era as a whole (defined in the sense of its essential contradictions), but are mainly embodied in the liberation movements which oppose capitalism, not in capitalism itself. Of course, in the spirit of the negation of the negation, what capitalism negates it also, in a sense, carries forward ("sublates" in Hegel's terminology), *but only as its own opposite*.

MORGAN AND THE "ORIGINS OF THE FAMILY"

On the question of dubious theories of historical stages, we have already mentioned the uncomfortable implications of Lewis Morgan's historicism in contributing to the justification of genocide. It will now be necessary for us to analyse Marx and Engels' attitude to Morgan.

Marx and Engels were both extremely interested in, and excited by, Morgan's work. This is partly explicable by his stance as a social radical: he held that capitalism had in some sense messed things up, and understood that there was something worthwhile in traditional society (in this case, Native American) which could be restored when capitalism was itself negated in favour of a better system. That looks like beautiful dialectics — only, unfortunately, it doesn't compensate for the racist elements in Morgan's thought. The last thing on Morgan's mind would be to say that Native American *resistance* movements are conveying the cause of progress; they would indeed be reactionary if they held up the unilinear progress, which must go through capitalism, and then beyond it. Indeed, he believed that social progress (through capitalism and beyond) was being propelled by a superior *people*, the so-called Aryans. It is relevant to note that the Aryan race-myth was subsequently developed by German Nazis who likewise claimed to transcend capitalism and restore the harmony of the tribe. Such an interpenetration between supposedly progressive and ultra-reactionary ideas is, and remains, complex, and we can use the Marxist method to guide us through this minefield (both in studying problems of historical analysis, and in formulating a political response to today's challenges, when issues are in many ways similar). Marx and Engels could have done so, but, owing to their Eurocentric limitations, often failed.

After Marx's death, Engels built upon the extensive discussions he had been holding with Marx about Morgan's work, as a central element in his important book *The Origins of the Family, Private Property and the State*. This book of Engels' presents quite a paradoxical character. At one level, in a remarkable contribution to human thought he proposed, decades ahead of its time, a vision of social history built essentially on the exploitation of women. This illustrates the potential of Marxism to encompass forms of superexploitation not entirely determined by class: from this aspect the book is a showcase for the theory's creativity.

But this only casts into sharper relief Engels' serious shortcomings, most notably in his failure to extend this brilliant paradigm of not-fully-class-based superexploitation to peoples of colour. In fact, the final section of this work presents itself as an extraordinary exercise in denial. As a focal point, in summing up his own argument and pointing the way to the future, Engels chooses to quote "in conclusion, Morgan's verdict on civilisation"; he thus groups together Morgan's statements from his own concluding section, making prophecies about how society will rise above private property and institute a new era of democracy, brotherhood, and equality.[21] Apparently the normative vision of communism is here given a scientific basis. But if one compares the passage as it appears in *The Origins of the Family* to Morgan's original, it is clear that Engels has merely censored out those parts where Morgan gives vent to the Aryan myth, *but without critiquing them*. It is impossible not to conclude that Marx and Engels were deliberately or subconsciously shutting their eyes to the reality which was going on all around them, i.e. the elaboration of what was to become the race-doctrine. They were simply too embarrassed or insecure to apply their own method to what should probably have been its most important task. Ideas which see history as a conflict between races (or "families" in Morgan's terminology) *cannot be defeated by ignoring them* or pretending they don't exist. While totally false, such ideas don't come from nowhere. This reflects in a distorted and wrong way the reality that capitalism has engendered a conflict between societies and nations in which the colonial peoples suffer racist oppression. This contradiction has to be faced up to squarely, rather than leaving the terrain to the racists.

DÜHRING'S STRUGGLE AGAINST NATURE

So were Marx and Engels so naive as to be misled by Morgan's "socialist" pretensions? That would be quite strange. They above all were experienced and sharp in detecting reaction dressed up as progress; didn't Engels rightly say that they had "fought harder all one's life long against self-styled Socialists than against anyone else"?[22] But the fact is, as far as the colonial question is concerned, the lines of demarcation for this "fight" were not well drawn. To illustrate this further, let's consider a case where Engels *did* polemicise against a self-styled socialist: his book *Anti-Dühring*.

Eugen Dühring was a German writer whose weird ideas, masquerading as socialism, were confusing the workers' movement at the time. Engels wanted to write a systematic presentation of the fundamental principles of Marxism in a lively way, and conceived the idea—since critique is often a good form of exposition—to do this by taking Dühring as negative teaching material. Now, Dühring was a bombastic egomaniac which made him an easy target. But there is something else as well: he was a leading racist. What could be more convenient than to take him as negative teaching material on this issue too? But this is just what Engels fails to do. Such was his denial that even after Dühring had published a book entirely devoted to propagating racism,[23] one which is considered by many as the direct precursor of Hitlerite antisemitism and national socialism, Engels saw fit to protest against the "despicable injustice" of the University of Berlin in sacking him![24] Engels' book therefore in no way *addresses* the issue of racism. Just as in his treatment of Morgan in *The Origins of the Family*, it is an exercise in denial. But things have a tendency to peep through, in the very act of denial itself. In this sense, the racism issue does indeed keep raising its head in *Anti-Dühring* in a way which, in fact, Engels himself fails to perceive.

One of Dühring's central themes is the so-called "struggle against nature," typical of the mechanical materialist view which sees the natural world as the enemy. The view is anti-ecological but at the same time Eurocentric, and the relationship between the two elements is important. In a general sense, the two are related because the reactionary "struggle against nature" idea negates all the achievements of traditional societies in building a harmonious relationship with the natural world, and the relevance of their experience for a future, post-capitalist system. More specifically, the struggle of colonialism to "master" nature has in fact always been (as we have argued, the notion of "virgin lands" being a myth) a struggle also to dispossess or enslave the people who were present in those lands and had learned to nurture their resources. These are errors which the dialectical perspective of Marxism is in principle ideally placed to criticise, but this is a task which Engels wholly fails to address.

Dühring's choice of image to express his theme is a very interesting one: once again, the story of *Robinson Crusoe*. As we showed earlier, *Crusoe* is in essence a colonial myth, showing how the superior intelligence of a man bred in the European environment allows him to tame and bend to his will both the savage *environment* of the tropics, and also the savage, the "native," himself. This myth has deep significance in the history of ideas, revealing as it does the centrality of the colonial experience within the mindset of "progressive" capitalism: a bit like racism itself, just because it's absurd doesn't mean it's unimportant, quite the opposite. But Engels wholly fails to perceive this, merely referring, dismissively, to the story as one which "properly belongs to the nursery and not to the field of science."[25] He does nevertheless analyse it, but in a strikingly inadequate way. He does so by treating *Crusoe* as a paradigm of *class* domination, saying that Dühring is wrong to see dominance as originating in an act of grabbing, rather than in the historical development of class society. This wholly misses the point—both of what Dühring was trying to argue, and of the unconscious assumptions underpinning his choice of metaphor. In reality, when we speak of colonialism, robbery *is* a valid concept, but this in no way contradicts the fact that a *continuing* exploitative system could only have been built if the robbery was in the last analysis an expression of the laws of capital accumulation, rather than an isolated act. Interestingly, Marx himself had earlier addressed the *Crusoe* narrative.[26] In a way, Marx's use of the narrative is better than Engels' because Marx did correctly highlight the aspect of the dominance over nature; but the indigenous population is forgotten, leaving us simply with a rehash of the virgin lands myth.

THE IMPORTANCE OF SOLIDARITY WITH LIBERATION MOVEMENTS

It is obvious that debates about the historic role of capitalism — progressive or otherwise — with respect to colonial peoples are not just theoretical: they reflect a constant need to respond politically to the choices which world politics constantly causes us to confront: do we shut our eyes to the real struggles, or take a stand?

Marx often did take a stand in condemning the atrocities committed by colonialism (albeit sometimes an inadequate one, if it meant merely condemning the *means* and not the objective result), but clearly the really big issue is: what stance to take about resistance, the fight back? That is the real touchstone. We should first make a few points to explain *why* resistance should be seen as progressive. We may pose the question, could anti-colonial resistance ever be a *bad* thing?

In answering this, the starting point is to repudiate linear ways of thinking. For example, even an argument like Rosa Luxemburg's, for all its insights, might be pushed to reactionary conclusions: if the breakdown of natural, non-commodity systems is intrinsic to capitalist development, this process would — by the *future* scope for the spread of accumulation into new terrain — exhaust the developmental potential of capitalism itself, and hasten its doom. Logically, one might say on this basis that there was no point delaying such a desirable outcome by encouraging resistance.

We can escape this problem by employing dialectics. What the linear reasoning forgets, first of all, is that what really follows from the breakdown of functioning social systems is not the enlargement of pure capitalist relations, but rather a dualistic system wherein the peripheries are kept in a situation of superexploited limbo, robbed of their traditional order but unable to generate a functioning new one. This issue was eventually explained by the dependency theory of the 1970s. And, secondly, linear reasoning ignores that the resistance movement, which may be partly a defence of the communal aspect of non-capitalist society, is what actually creates the experimentation for a new social order. For both these reasons, national struggles remain progressive throughout the different stages of capitalism.

In the modernisation myth, capitalism offers a benign embrace within which all peoples can find their place. Whenever Eurocentrism distances itself from an exclusionist form of racism (according to which subject peoples are uncivilisable because they are designated as genetically inferior) it inevitably falls into assimilationism. Today's "globalisation" discourse is merely the latest expression. In fact, even if we take assimilationism at face value, it is reactionary and absurd: it would lead straight to homogenisation, to an abolition of the *variety* of responses to the natural environment acquired within different national and local cultures, a diversity essential to provide humanity with a wide vocabulary of responses to possibly unforeseen problems. But of course, assimilation does not even bring a genuine homogenisation, it is actually worse: it denies what might theoretically be the only good aspect of homogenisation—equality! The reference point around which things are homogenised is always the culture of the oppressor, the denial of that of the oppressed.

In response to assimilation-homogenisation, the liberation movements assert their own particularity, but this itself serves as the basis for a higher unity because the liberation movement is a global current synthesising within itself the concrete richness of different cultures and thus creating a movement for the whole of humanity for the first time. In the pre-capitalist era, while there was constant cross-fertilisation between different cultures, there was still no single current of human history. Capitalism negated this situation at the price of bringing about far more acute divisions, particularly racist exploitation, than were seen in any previous era. But the *resistance* this process produces, in the context of a single world system of production, creates the possibility of negating these divisions and moving to a new, more integrated stage in human history, sharing and universalising the *whole* range of human responses to our environment. The idea that the capitalist era heralds a new epoch of progress is indisputably correct, but only in the sense that the revolutionary movements which *negate* capitalism (although in this very negation they can subsume, in a changed form, some things which have developed during the capitalist epoch, for example aspects of its technology) become the sole forces embodying this progressive potential. The deduction from the above argument is simple: solidarity with the liberation movements. The above is a theoretical response but, in fact, radicals should also have a gut instinct telling them to applaud and declare solidarity with acts of resistance.

So where did Marx and Engels stand on this crucial issue? A useful entry-point is to consider the relationship between the condemnation of colonial atrocities and support for resistance. Mao Zedong formulated the relationship correctly: while we wholly condemn imperialist wars, we can nevertheless sense that they bring a progressive future closer—not of course by promoting some linear historical progression through stages of capitalism, but because of the creative force generated by the resistance to which they give rise. But Marx and Engels found it hard to push the reasoning to this conclusion. On the one hand, it is important to recognise that they did not stint in condemning massacres. Thus, on Algeria, Engels writes:

> From the first occupation of Algeria by the French to the present time, the unhappy country has been the arena of unceasing bloodshed, rapine and violence. Each town, large and small, has been conquered in detail at an immense sacrifice of life. The Arab and Kabyle tribes, to whom independence is precious, and hatred of foreign domination a principle dearer than life itself, have been crushed and broken by the terrible razzias in which dwellings and property are burnt and destroyed, standing crops cut down, and the miserable wretches who remain massacred, or subjected to all the horrors of lust and brutality.[27]

And, if anything, their condemnations of the British army in India were even harsher.

But, on the other hand, there was a certain tendency to distinguish between condemnation of the horrendous *means* employed in colonialist invasions or occupations, and somehow a more nuanced appraisal of the objective result. Even if we lay aside the complex dialectical reasoning, the gut instinct should surely show you this is wrong: if in every case the means seem to be atrocious, might we not suspect that the act itself is inherently atrocious? Somehow Marx and Engels mostly failed to make this deduction; which in turn makes it hard to come to a principled stance of support for the forces of opposition, the actual popular struggle as a thing in and for itself with its own intrinsic interests, justification, and creativity.

A typical instance which demands closer study is Engels' article "Details of the Attack on Lucknow" (1858). The article roundly condemns the British Army's "plundering, violence, massacre," ironises about "their civilising and humanising progress through India,"[28] but is at the same time full of superior and patronising references to the Indians. Marx and Engels never wholly surmounted the view that colonialism, however regrettable for its atrocities, was still objectively a force for progress. They didn't recognise that the only progressive legacy of colonialism is the resistance against it.

THE POTENTIAL FOR DEVELOPMENT OUTSIDE EUROPE

The above issues are closely linked to the question of the developmental potential of non-European societies. Dialectics should teach one that everything is in constant change and flux: such was the worldview of the pre-Socratic thinkers (based in ancient Greece but heavily influenced by Eastern thought) who passed on their dialectics to Hegel, and through Hegel, Marx. But somehow Marx and Engels had a strong tendency to look at non-European society and see stagnation—if this was the case colonialism could presumably not lead to blocked development because there would be nothing to block! We can examine this problem by considering Marx's letter to Engels in June 14, 1853. The Moscow publication *On Colonialism*, a collection of writings by Marx and Engels, carries extracts from this letter, among them the following passage addressing the question of the traditional Indian system of self-contained village communities:

> I do not think anyone could imagine a more solid foundation for a stagnant Asiatic despotism. And however much the English may have hibernicised the country, the breaking up of these stereotyped primitive forms was the sine qua non for Europeanisation ... The destruction of their archaic industry was necessary to deprive the villages of their self-supporting character.[29]

This clearly implies that Europeanisation is a good and necessary thing and is equated with progress.

In fact the editors of *On Colonialism* were a bit selective; they omitted another passage in the same letter, in which Marx makes this argument still more sharply. In this passage, Marx refers approvingly to a claim in a book by Carey, *Slavery at Home and Abroad*, to the effect that

> the main body of Negroes in Jamaica, etc., always consist of newly-imported barbarians, as under English

treatment the Negroes were not only unable to maintain their population but always two-thirds of the number annually imported lost their lives; the present generation of Negroes in America, on the other hand, is becoming a native product, more or less Yankeefied, English-speaking, etc., and therefore *fit for emancipation*.[30]

This implies that the slaves must first accept brainwashing by European culture in order to be fit to be free (or rather to *be freed*, as objects). Here again, Europeanisation is regarded as a virtue. It is rather reprehensible that Marx should support such an argument. It is also quite telling in relation to his response to the practical political choices of the day: if slaves in the USA had supposedly been "Yankeefied" in a nice way, where does this leave Black people in the Caribbean, who were presumably still imbued with African cultures?

As we have said, slave revolts in the Caribbean were among the most spectacular liberation struggles of the early capitalist period—and the bourgeoisie made no mistake about their significance, they were trembling with fear. More specifically, in 1856 Paul Bogle led a revolutionary uprising in Jamaica and the British colonialists unleashed a barbaric reign of terror in attempting to suppress it. This was a period when racist ideology was striving to win hegemony over the hearts and minds of the working class, but there was still considerable working-class sympathy for the oppressed[31] and this could have provided a basis for political work by the left.

But this opportunity was ignored by Marx and Engels. Despite widespread debate within society, they thought they knew better: supposedly the struggles had no future because there was nothing they could draw from their own intrinsic roots which could establish their historical validity. In a letter to Marx dated December 1, 1865, Engels, far from expressing solidarity with the revolutionary struggle, merely remarks in passing about the atrocities committed against "unarmed Niggers";[32]

this is practically like reporting British colonialism to the Royal Society for the Prevention of Cruelty to Animals for whipping a dumb cur.

Yet these same Africans were the people who had proudly risen up and established liberated areas in the heart of Jamaica — among the first such areas in the history of the anti-colonial movement — which the British could never subdue by force of arms. In Haiti the slaves had established their own independent state and their famous leaders won a grudging respect, even from the bourgeoisie, for their superb military and political skill.

It is not just that these struggles were "deserving of support" in the sense that they required sympathy, rather that they were offering a lead: they were indicating the direction in which history was moving, or should move. And if that direction was not yet clear to the workers' movement in general, that is all the more reason for valuing the vanguard role of such liberation movements. In fact they point in the direction of something which was to become an outstanding theme of the twentieth century: people's war — it will be interesting to explore briefly the implications of this concept.

Engels, building on a certain Germanic tradition, had a big interest in the history and technique of warfare. This could have opened up possibilities of great value to the communist movement: after all, so much of the international history of the imperialist era was to be driven by the clash between imperialist repression and popular resistance. The colonial era in which Engels was writing anticipated many of these issues, and it would have been precious had he left us with the outlines of a historical materialist theory of the evolution of people's war against the background of earlier military theory.

In a certain respect, the objective historic process did push its way into Engels' consciousness, but the Eurocentric framework of his thought was such that it could neither contain, nor be broken apart by, these epic changes. Therefore, his thinking often possesses a self-contradictory character that *reflects* the reality to some extent, but shrinks from drawing the required conclusions. Such contradictions are illustrated rather well in an article written earlier than *Anti-Dühring*, called "Persia-China":

> In short, instead of moralising on the horrible atrocities of the Chinese, as the chivalrous English press does, we had better recognise this is a war *pro aris et focis*, a popular war for the maintenance of Chinese nationality, with all its overbearing prejudice, stupidity, learned ignorance and pedantic barbarism if you like but yet a popular war. And in a popular war the means used by the insurgent nation cannot be measured by the commonly recognised rules of regular warfare, nor by any other abstract standard, but by the degree of civilisation only attained by that insurgent nation.[33]

This passage unquestionably hints at a progressive potential, in particular a farsighted perception of the concept of people's war and an affirmation of the right to struggle by any means necessary; but combined with a Eurocentric prejudice, it also demonstrates stupidity and learned ignorance regarding Chinese civilisation. Thus, Engels assumes that the barbaric character of the war was determined by the limitations of *Chinese* society, not by the barbarism of the colonialist! There is a certain implication of mechanical materialism, if it is assumed that European society has progressed in such a manner as to leave that barbarism behind. The uneasy contradictoriness of such a position is such that it is hardly surprising that it was not sustainable. Engels resolved it by dropping one side of the contradiction—unfortunately it was the progressive side!

Thus, returning again to *Anti-Dühring*, Engels took the opportunity (as part of his plan to use that book as a kind of manual of Marxist theory) to produce what was meant to be an extensive historical-materialist account of warfare, using all the research he had gleaned.[34] But in place of the dialectical tensions of the previous passage, he simply ditched his earlier and correct views about people's war and ignored the subject altogether. As Fanon has pointed out, the military chapter in that book is quite mechanical;[35] the reason is not hard to understand. In the case of white people waging the American "war of independence" (people who were fighting the colonial power while at the same time were *themselves* colonizers waging genocidal war against the indigenous population as well as practising slavery), Engels *does* recognise that subjective factors ("they were fighting for their vital interests")[36] can prevail over superior objective military strength (one of the tenets of people's war); but he has nothing to say about the subjective factor in liberation wars in the wider colonial context, nor indeed about the powerful objective force unleashed by an oppressed society in revolt, however ground-down this society may have appeared to be. This is another good illustration of the organic link between Eurocentrism and mechanical materialism. Marx and Engels did not fully realise that the more humanity is oppressed and denied, the more explosively it asserts itself.

Again, this takes us back to the question of the historicity of non-European peoples. It should be noted that oppressed peoples should not in any case be obligated to demonstrate their historicity as a condition for the recognition of their humanity or human rights. But in any case, they *do* have a place within the time-frame of human existence, linking the achievements of their cultural past with the future cause of revolution.

When Marx and Engels considered the prevailing situation in "uncivilised" countries brutish, we can consider this true only in terms of the oppressive structures, particularly the colonial ones, which are indeed brutish, and not in terms of the oppressed. Of course, aspects of traditional indigenous society are indeed oppressive—with respect to women, for example—there is class stratification, and even the humanity of certain groups may be denied, as with the caste system. But the whole point is that liberation struggles cannot be led to victory from above. Imperialist exploitation tends to build upon, and develop symbiotically with, indigenous forms of oppression and exploitation, and ultimately those whom the system most often seeks to dehumanise become the leading force in destroying this same system—a necessary step so that their humanity can emerge. This will necessarily include settling accounts with the internal, oppressive, and dehumanising elements within their own societies. It is a revolutionary paradox that liberation movements unleash the forces, especially women and the peasant masses, that were ground down even by the traditional system and, while these movements still necessarily retain a national character in order to fight the racial-colonialist dominance of the North, in a larger sense they drive forward the contradiction between the irrepressible humanity of the most oppressed and the different systemic forms of oppression.

MARX AND ENGELS' SUBORDINATION OF THE NATIONAL QUESTION

In general Marx and Engels' position on the national question was to subordinate it to the supposed interests of the proletariat. On the one hand, national movements were only valid if those nations could themselves produce a proletariat, and on the other hand they were supported only insofar as they concretely promoted the interests of the proletarian movement in the "advanced" countries. On the first of these two aspects Engels, in particular, adhered to the idea that those peoples who could not by themselves produce a bourgeoisie, and hence a proletariat, were "history-less":

> These relics of a nation mercilessly trampled under foot in the course of history, as Hegel says, these *residual fragments of peoples* always become the fanatical standard-bearers of counter-revolution, and remain so until their complete extirpation or loss of their national character[37]

This is genocidal in its implication. The examples Engels gives in the article from which the above quotation is taken are of European peoples (such as the Gaels of Scotland, the Bretons, the Basques, and the South Slavs), but in a certain sense this entire perspective—which cheerfully contemplates the extermination of inconvenient nationalities—springs from colonial experience. The colonial peoples, more than any others, were considered "history-less" (according to the imposed Eurocentric definition), and therefore lacking any *future* viability. It appears as though, in a manner perilously close to the passage we quoted earlier from Morgan, one particular group of humanity possesses the monopoly over the mainstream of social progress. The particular "Aryan" framework in which Morgan expressed this notion is not affirmed by the founders of Marxism, but neither is it repudiated. The paradox is that, within Marxism, this dangerous position co-existed with, and was by a strange logic supposed to be compatible with, an immensely progressive stance when it came to attacking any form of national oppression carried out under the guise of revolution.

In 1847, right at the beginning of their career, Marx and Engels stated unequivocally that "a nation cannot become free and at the same time continue to oppress other nations" and, more specifically, that "Revolutionary Germany ... must, along with its own freedom, proclaim the freedom of the peoples which it has hitherto oppressed."[38] The importance of these principled positions must be emphasised; indeed, professional anti-communists like Carlos Moore, as we will observe later, go to great pains to conceal them. The fact is that Marx and Engels are clearly differentiated from the social-chauvinism which infected the communist movement in the pre-Lenin period and which crept back gradually after Lenin's death.

At the same time, however, the limitations of Marx and Engels' position must also be admitted. The leading factor in the revolution was definitely understood to be the proletariat of the advanced countries—it was not in *their* interest to oppress other nations. Although this position is correct, and indeed highly important, it is not the same as recognising that the oppressed have their own interests.

There is also a certain tendency in such statements to speak of the advanced proletariat as being able to *free* the oppressed peoples (as objects) rather than the latter being capable of freeing themselves (as in the notion, "we are our own liberators"). This was admittedly not always the case, and in many instances Marx and Engels did recognise that oppressed peoples were struggling for their own freedom; therefore, since the advanced proletariat had an interest in getting rid of national oppression, struggles for national liberation should be supported. But in this context such support was selective because it was determined by what was conceived to be the interest of the proletariat of the advanced capitalist countries. The chauvinism which later developed in the workers' movement, while at one level in total contradiction to the correct principles laid down by Marx, was at the same time not entirely disconnected from the "superior" attitude which he cultivated in judging national movements. For example, in a letter to Engels on December 1, 1851, Marx congratulates himself on the fact that Ernest Jones, the English Chartist, had—on Marx's prompting—referred in the following terms to the Hungarian revolutionary leader, Kossuth:

> I tell him, that the revolutions of Europe mean the crusade of labour against capital, and I tell him they are not to be cut to the intellectual and social standard of an obscure semi-barbarous people like the Magyars, still standing in the half-civilisation of the sixteenth century, who actually presume to dictate to the great enlightenment of Germany and France, and to gain a false won cheer from the gullibility of England.[39]

ANALYSIS OF THE INTERNATIONAL RELATIONS SYSTEM

Another major expression of Eurocentrism arises in the field of international politics. Here, the significant error is to overemphasise conflicts amongst European powers at the expense of the wider reality of world affairs, which was the colonial expansion beyond Europe. This error also finds a certain basis in Marx and Engels' thinking. There were national struggles that they strongly supported, particularly the national struggle in Poland, but this support depended on an analysis of the international situation in which the cause of progress was strongly focused on the agenda in Europe—in particular the need for the proletariat to defeat bastions of reaction. Thus, for example: "The partition of Poland is the cement which binds together the great military despotisms: Russia, Prussia and Austria. Only the restoration of Poland can break this bond and thus liquidate the greatest obstacle to the emancipation of the European peoples."[40]

The starting point—and here Marx and Engels were obviously correct—was that the ruling classes of Europe would not allow revolutions to run their course in a particular country: they would mobilise internationally to prevent such situations. But to present this understanding as the central issue in international relations at a *world* level is problematical. This Eurocentric reasoning crops up in a somewhat bizarre form in Marx's interesting and rarely studied work on international politics, the *Secret Diplomatic History of the Eighteenth Century*,[41] which generally implies that the whole of world history revolved around the international threat from the reactionary Russian regime; those national movements which might serve to hold it in check should be backed.

Yet, to put it mildly, Russian politics was not the totality, or even the most significant aspect, of eighteenth-century international relations. Even mainstream thinking recognised the colonial dimension of the wars between European states (France, Spain, England, etc.); now, Marx was presumably trying to correct a certain superficiality in this emphasis on conflicting

European nationalisms by revealing the existence of a hidden war aimed at suppressing social progress that was using the reactionary semi-feudal Russian regime as its spearhead. This could be quite an interesting insight, but it is weakened by the fact that Marx, in this context, fails to see that the colonial wars were themselves only superficially a product of rivalry between conflicting European nationalisms: in a deeper sense they reflected a kind of collective expansion of white power at the expense of the rest of humanity. The cause of progress cannot possibly be formulated in such a way as to sideline this issue.

As C.L.R. James has shown, the struggle over the slave trade and over the zones of production was of absolute and primordial importance for international and domestic affairs in Europe.[42] Moreover, as James also correctly states—and this might seem obvious, but curiously it needed to be said—the struggle was (legitimately) of primordial importance to the slaves themselves! The Haitian struggle was revolutionary in its own right, and thus possessed the absolute right to choose its own methods, tactics, and alliances. The alliance with the French Revolution was only conditional on the latter favouring the emancipation of slaves. This, then, was a redefinition of the reality of international affairs through practice: through the practice of struggling peoples, conveyed through great sacrifices and with great ingenuity. Such a perspective not only corrects the narrow, Eurocentric view of a world politics revolving around central Europe but also, and more profoundly, critiques the assumption that liberation movements had no *intrinsic* interests and autonomy beyond that conferred by their value to the most "advanced" revolutions in Europe.

Marx and Engels' system of ideas was not static. In contrast to the mechanical position—that England, with its most advanced capitalist relations, would also necessarily be advanced in revolutionary terms—they began to understand that the colonial relationship was producing the opposite result, i.e. depressing revolution in the core nations. When writing, for example, "with the drain of men and bullion which it must cost the English,

India is now our best ally,"[43] they are already demonstrating the recognition that the periphery could have an impact *upon* the centre. Nevertheless, this insight is still compatible with the Eurocentric perspective of giving primacy to the core proletariat's interests. On the Irish question they pushed the boundaries of their thought even further, recognising that England's colonial relationship with Ireland bolstered the ruling order and helped to defuse the workers' movement—not just in an economic sense, but politically and ideologically as well: revolution in Ireland would disrupt this cosy, torpid equilibrium. This was an immensely progressive and important stance. Even so, here too the framework was still that the metropolitan proletarian movement was the primary historical force, and other national struggles were positive if they helped this cause. They spelled this out with extreme logical clarity in the following statement dating from 1870:

> England, being the metropolis of capital, the power which has hitherto ruled the world market, is for the present the most important country for the workers' revolution, and moreover the *only* country in which the material conditions for this revolution have developed up to a certain degree of maturity. Therefore to hasten the social revolution in England is the most important object of the International Workingmen's Association. The sole means of hastening it is to make Ireland independent.[44]

WAS ENGELS A RACIST?

To conduct a critique of Marx and Engels' positions demonstrates the dynamism of dialectical materialism. On the basis of such an analysis, we can highlight the fundamentally correct core of the Marxist legacy while at the same time pinpointing the contextual limitations—limitations that would subsequently lead to the degeneration of the communist movement in some regions, while being resisted in others. In making this critique, we demarcate ourselves from commentators like Carlos Moore, who exploit the real Eurocentric and racist weaknesses of Marx and Engels in order to reinforce the anti-communist agenda of the ruling system.[45] As an example, it is instructive to examine two of Engels' letters, both written in 1882. The first of these passages is quoted by Carlos Moore in his attack on Marx and Engels, but in a selective manner which deliberately distorts and manipulates its meaning. In the following extract we place in bold the passages omitted by Moore:

> **You ask me what the English workers think about colonial policy. Well, exactly the same as they think about politics in general: the same as the bourgeois think. There is no worker's party here, you see, there are only Conservatives and Liberal-Radicals, and the workers gaily share the feast of England's monopoly of the world market and the colonies.** In my opinion the colonies proper, i.e. the countries occupied by a European population—Canada, the Cape, Australia—will all become independent; on the other hand, the countries inhabited by a native population, which are simply subjugated—India, Algeria, the Dutch, Portuguese and Spanish possessions—must be taken over for the time being by the proletariat and led as rapidly as possibly towards independence. How this process will develop is difficult to say. **India will perhaps, indeed very probably, make a revolution and as a proletariat in process of self-emancipation cannot conduct any colonial wars, it would have to be allowed to run its course; it would not pass off without all sorts of destruction, of course, but that sort of thing is inseparable from all revolutions. The same might also take place elsewhere, e.g. in Algeria or Egypt, and**

would certainly be the best thing for us. We shall have enough to do at home. Once Europe is reorganised, and North America, that will furnish such colossal power and such an example, that the semi-civilised countries will of themselves follow in their wake; economic needs, if anything, will see to that. But as to what social and political phases these countries will then have to pass through before they likewise arrive at socialist organisation, I think we today can advance only rather idle hypotheses. One thing alone is certain: the victorious proletariat can force no blessings of any kind upon any foreign nation without undermining its own victory by doing so. Which of course by no means excludes defensive wars of various kinds.[46]

In the spirit of seeking a genuinely historical materialist critique of Marx and Engels, it is important to emphasise that we are not claiming the ideas laid out in the bold passages are absolutely correct, simply that they are essential if we are to make a scientific appraisal of Engels' position, and thus advance revolutionary theory in the process. Engels recognises that the actually-existing workers' movement is completely within the framework of bourgeois ideology on the colonial question: this is an extremely important and correct analysis, one which the communist movement would later and unfortunately abandon. **Since its enslavement to the bourgeoisie on the colonial question is a condition for the proletariat's enslavement in general**, any movements which help rid the proletariat of this burden are a good thing. Moore's distortion of the passage gives the impression that Marx and Engels were social-colonialists which is entirely false.

At the same time, the limitations in Engels' position are clear. The situation is explicitly assessed according to what is best *for us* — i.e., the metropolitan workers' movement. Despite the claim to internationalism, Engels is not including the colonial peoples among this *us*. Instead, the leading force in the future epoch of world history (not just the history of Europe but the history of the rest of the world) is still assumed to be Europe, now rationally organised under proletarian leadership. From this analysis there follows logically a certain stance on anti-colonial solidarity which is quite problematical. Under the auspices of being "materialist" and hard-headed, shunning idealism, Engels does not shrink from a stark articulation of this view, as in the following extract from his letter to Bernstein of August 9, 1882:

> We Western-Europeans should not be so easily led astray as the Egyptian fellahs or all the Romanic people. All the Romanic revolutionaries complain that all the revolutions they have made were always for the benefit of other people. This is easily explained: it is because they were always taken in by the word "revolution." And yet, no sooner a mutiny breaks out somewhere, then the entire Romanic revolutionary world is in rapture over it uncritically. I think that we can well be on the side of the oppressed fellahs without sharing the illusions they nurture at the time (a peasant people just has to be hoodwinked for centuries before it becomes aware of it from experience), and to be **against the English brutalities while by no means siding with their military adversaries of the moment**. In all questions of international politics the sentimental party newspapers of the French and Italians are to be used with the utmost mistrust, and we Germans are duty-bound to preserve our theoretical superiority through criticism in this sphere as well.[47]

Thus, support is withheld from the actual resistance struggles whenever they allegedly represent dead-end social and economic forces.

THE PROGRESSIVE POTENTIAL
OF MARXIST POLITICAL ECONOMY

Such selectiveness is what stands in the way of Marxism expanding its compass to address all of the world's peoples. This is what must be overcome. Since objectively Marx and Engels were the progenitors of the most revolutionary ideology ever, it is not surprising that, even within the somewhat Eurocentric framework of the *origins* of their thought, the most farsighted concepts kept pushing their way through. Thus, for example, the following statement from 1858: "Is it [the socialist revolution] not bound to be crushed in this little corner [Europe], considering that in a far greater territory the movement of bourgeois society is still on the ascendant?"[48]

This perspective is extremely farsighted, and opens up an understanding of how capital was later able to surmount the crisis of the '20s and '30s and even create an unexpected boom, first in 1945 and then in 1980: had the Soviets taken this insight seriously they would not have been spouting nonsense even as their system went to its doom. The point is the potential for capital accumulation through heightened superexploitation and the cultivation of dependent development in the colonies and neo-colonies. We can understand how this happened by applying Marxism in a non-Eurocentric way—as, for example, Samir Amin would eventually do by showing that the consolidation of the core was achieved because the tendency to pauperise the workers, predicted by Marx as a necessary tendency of capitalism, is in a sense exported to the dependent economies of the neo-colonial countries.[49]

Because Marx and Engels were very close to the revolutionary movement in Ireland, and in a sense articulated the objective and subjective strength of that movement through their work, they produced certain ideas in this context which have applicability to the whole colonial situation. In one remarkable passage Marx even hints at the way capitalism creams off the surplus from primary accumulation in the colonies—thus limiting the possibility for indigenous development—at the export of pauperisation, at the development of underdevelopment; he even penetratingly criticises the colonial ideology (complete with its racial stereotypes) which protects the entire system:

> [A] class of absentee landlords has been enabled to pocket not merely the labour but also the capital of whole generations, each generation of Irish peasants sinking a grade lower in the social scale, exactly in proportion to the exertions and sacrifices made for the raising of their condition and that of their families. If the tenant was industrious and enterprising, he became taxed in consequence of his very industry and enterprise. If, on the contrary, he grew inert and negligent, he was reproached with the "aboriginal faults of the Celtic race."[50]

It is worth asking whether Marx and Engels' thought underwent an evolution over time from less correct to more correct positions on the question of *non-European* peoples' struggles. In our view, it would be too simplistic to assume a smooth or linear progression in this sense.[51] Nevertheless, there was what we could call a "reaching-out," on Marx and Engels' part, in the direction of a truly universalist application of dialectical and historical materialism that would embrace humanity as a whole. It was neither smooth nor linear but, despite some false turns and Eurocentric hangovers, there was indeed an evolution towards a deeper understanding, particularly on Marx's part.

MARX BEGINS TO CHALLENGE HIS EUROCENTRIC LIMITATIONS

Marx was continually trying to expand his horizons, and despite his illness, the pressure of work on *Capital*, and his practical involvement with the European workers' movement, he still devoted enormous energy to study in his final years—and probably the main topic upon which he focused was precisely to understand all he could about non-European peoples. His philosophy was, after all, founded on a respect for the dialectical laws of *material reality*, and he would be the first to recognise that ignorance of the facts would generate wrong theory.

Shortly before his death, for example, Marx compiled a huge volume of notes on a topic about which he had written extensively earlier, but on a basis of inadequate knowledge: India. Here, for instance, he gives an account of the emperor Akbar (1556–1605), mentioning the latter's religious tolerance, dedication to stamping out abuse by officials and the setting up of an effective legal system, and remarks that during this reign Delhi was made "into the greatest and finest city then existing in the world."[52] This is quite a different perspective from the image of mindless tyranny which tended to surface in his earlier views. He also exhibits a more dialectical attitude to *resistance*, appreciating the need to critique the distortions and vilification heaped upon Indian resistance by the colonisers. Referring ironically to the so-called Black Hole of Calcutta incident "over which the *English hypocrites* have been making so much sham scandal to this day," Marx remarks: **"Bengal is now completely and effectively cleared of the English intruders."**[53] In such statements, we find evidence that Marx was moving towards a recognition both of the intrinsic historical dynamic of Indian society and of the absolute justification of the liberation struggle, as well as the way colonial ideology manipulates the image of barbarism, transposing its own barbarism onto the people it brutalises. Also in his last years, Marx compiled volumes of notes from various ethnological works. In these notes he tries to learn from the concrete facts reported while making comments in which he ridicules the philistinism of the scholars who imagine that they are judging so-called inferior races from a high vantage point but are in fact simply exposing their own stupidity and prejudices.

An extremely interesting example of this, which actually casts the thinking of the late Marx in a completely new light, is a little-known text providing a critical commentary on Sir John Lubbock's *The Origin of Civilisation and the Primitive Condition of Man* (London, 1870). In these notes, he calls Lubbock a "civilised ass" for assuming that male inheritance is the norm against which other societies must be measured.[54] He quotes the passage "[i]ndeed the savage who worships an animal or a tree, would see no absurdity in worshipping a man" only to add his own note: "as if the civilised Englishman does not 'worship' the Queen or Mr. Gladstone."[55] The following is a typical passage from his synopsis of Lubbock's book, the bracketed phrases being Marx's humorous comments:

> D. Reverend Lang in his *"The Aborigines of Australia"* had a friend who "tried long and patiently to make a very intelligent Australian *understand* (sollte heißen make him believe) *his existence without a body*, but the black never would keep his countenance ... for a long time he could not believe ("he" is the intelligent black) that the "gentleman" (i.e. die Pfaffen Lang's silly friend) *was serious*, and when he did realise it (that the gentleman was an ass in good earnest), the more serious the teacher was, the more ludicrous the whole affair appeared to be (Spottet Lubbock seiner selbst u. weißt doch nicht wie).[56]

MARX'S VIEW OF STAGES

One of the most remarkable dialectical ideas which Marx developed was his view that societies could progress directly to socialism, on the basis of their surviving communal structure, without having to go through the intervening stage of capitalism. This insight completely breaks with the linear model which we critiqued earlier; it opens the way to a new social order organised through commons regimes. "Regime" in this sense means a mode of organisation. In pre-capitalist societies various resources, including physical ones like land but also (importantly) knowledge, were typically organised as commons, meaning that no one had the right individually to appropriate them. This demand often re-surfaced in revolutionary movements, for example, in England, the Diggers of 1649. Although superficially commons appear as a common means of management in the interest *of people*, in indigenous thinking this is always premised on a duty of stewardship with respect *to nature*: the regime has an absolute duty to prevent the resource being depleted (the management of grazing lands by traditional pastoralists being one example). Today's progressive social movements, for example in India and Bolivia, strongly emphasise this link between commons and ecological stewardship. Capitalism and colonialism have mostly vowed absolute hostility towards commons, promoting a frantic appropriation not just of land and resources, but of knowledge. Quite recently, in a bid to appropriate the value generated by society's self-organising capacities, we witness a subtle shift by the mainstream (exemplified by its enthusiasm for the work of economist Elinor Ostrom) to incorporate some tame aspects of commons management as a subordinate part of a political economy overwhelmingly dominated by private appropriation. But in a deep and strategic sense, commons remain antithetical to capitalism, and a bridge between the indigenous social systems and the communist vision derived from Marx and Engels.

An important ingredient in this concept was Marx's view on the question of the land. Here too we find interesting evidence of an evolution in his ideas. He initially thought that the lack of private property in land was a factor holding back progress[57] and that, consequently, colonialism could be progressive in the breaking up of traditional property relations, for example, in India. At the same time, and from very early on, Marx grasped the fact that the basis of the colonial contradiction lies in depriving the subject people of their own land. In the case of India, this theme comes across very strongly in an important article on the

Annexation of Oudh written in 1858[58] where, just as in the case of Ireland, Marx was "convinced from the first that the social revolution must begin seriously from the bottom, that is, from land ownership."[59]

Taking this one step further, Marx began to perceive a link between rural society and revolution. This understanding is completely different from a mechanical view which would neglect rural society in favour of advanced (urban) productive forces. In particular, Marx devoted great attention to studying Russia, and in doing so looked carefully at the views of the great revolutionary theoretician, Nicolai Chernyshevsky who had raised the following question: "Must Russia start, as her liberal economists wish, by destroying the village community so as to go over the capitalist system, or can she, without undergoing the torments of the system, secure all its fruits, while developing her own historical endowments?"[60]

In a letter to Vera Zasulich of March 8, 1881, Marx refers to the village community as a "strategic point of social regeneration" in Russia.[61] There was thus a possibility of using the village community as a basis for building an alternative society. The clear implication is that the destruction of traditional society by capitalism can no longer be seen as progressive.

This shift in Marx's ideas is extremely important since it anticipated, by at least a century, the debates regarding the role of commons regimes as the basis for an alternative social order while, at the same time, providing a dialectical framework within which to analyse these debates. Although worked out in relation to Russia, this theory had worldwide implications that Engels would later make explicit: "[The] abbreviated process of development ... applies not only to Russia but to all countries at the pre-capitalist stage of development."[62]

The way in which Engels developed this idea after Marx's death was, however, not wholly satisfactory. He fails to settle the historical question of how the stagnation of the colonial countries originated, tending to assume that their "abbreviated" development to socialism would occur not from their own intrinsic dynamic but only in response to an impetus from the metropolis. In an 1884 letter to Kautsky, Engels thus discusses the situation in Java (then a Dutch colony), describing

> how today primitive communism furnishes there as well as in India and Russia the finest and broadest basis of exploitation and despotism (so long as it is not aroused by some element of modern communism) and how in the conditions of modern society it turns out to be a crying anachronism (to be removed or further developed) as much as were the independent mark associations of the original cantons.[63]

While it is true that the deliberate maintenance of truncated pre-capitalist structures provides an essential basis for colonial (or neo-colonial) despotism—an idea developed in the 1950s writings of Paul Baran, a major precursor of dependency theory—we should identify the main culprit as traditional systems of *dominance* rather than traditional co-operative structures. Similarly, the notion of being "aroused" by modern communism carries with it the implication that metropolitan socialism must play a leading role. Such an assumption was spelled out even more clearly a decade later in Engels' afterword to his work *On Social Relations in Russia*: here the democratic traditions in non-centralised societies are seen as backward "relics," passively awaiting the kiss of life from the metropolitan proletariat:

> Only when the capitalist economy has been overcome at home and in the countries of its prime, only when the retarded countries have seen from their example "how it's done," how the productive forces of modern industry are made to work as social property for society as a whole—only then will the retarded countries be able to start on this abbreviated process of development. But then their success will be assured.[64]

Despite these limitations, it is obviously very significant that Marx and Engels came to understand that countries outside the heartland of capitalism could step directly into the front ranks of historical progress. The specific *form* on which they focused, the land question and peasant regimes, can probably be seen as just one aspect of a wider phenomenon, the striving of working people to relate to their own social and natural environment in a way which is in harmony with its objective laws: the principle of socio-institutional stewardship over natural resources through commons regimes keeps reasserting itself whether or not there is a direct link with its ancient traditional forms. Humanity is in essence social and seeks a sustainable relationship with its biosphere. This fact was expressed in communitarian land-tenure systems, but not *only* in that form—equally, it took a cultural form. It is not really a communal approach to land *ownership* but, rather, a culture which repudiates *any* ownership of land. Here we are addressing the widest sense in which social being determines consciousness, and this wider form existed on a very long time-scale, reaching across major changes in modes of production and social formations.

Pre-colonial class societies grafted themselves on top of these productive and institutional structures, cultures and traditions, extracting tribute without calling into question their continued existence (which would have been nonsense if they formed the continuing basis of the tribute!). However, there was not only harmony in these societies, but also contradiction, and this was precisely the basis of their dynamism. There was certainly at times a tendency to undermine the social basis of harmony with the natural world by extracting too large a tribute. Hence the democratic nature of peasant society also had a political dimension—it was asserted against tyranny. Without these contradictions, the societies would have been stagnant. Chinese historians, for example, have illustrated the dynamic function of peasant rebellions within the context of exploiting-class society and, in this sense, the democratic struggles of the labouring people are always progressive. But before the advent of capitalism it was impossible for these struggles fundamentally to change the system itself and set up a new mode of production; at most they could, as in Imperial China, overthrow one dynasty and allow for the founding of another. The mass movement had thus always been an integral part of the dynamism within all societies; what changed with the advent of capitalism was that the cause of the masses acquired for the first time a realisable form.

Such ideas were certainly bubbling somewhere within Marx's thinking, chipping away at the edifice of linearity and Eurocentrism. They can provide us with a key to understanding wider problems of the relationship between national liberation, the natural world, and socialism. Ultimately, what has propelled us, within the movement, towards a better understanding has been revolutionary practice. Thus, the image of isolated communities of peasants with horizons limited to the village—which we find in the more unsatisfactory formulations of Marx and Engels ("[s]uch a complete isolation of the individual communities from one another, which creates throughout the country similar, but the very opposite of common, interests"[65])—was refuted in the colonial period when widespread resistance movements developed rapidly. In India, resistance flared up over large areas on many occasions from the latter part of the eighteenth century onwards and was creative in its exploration of methods of armed struggle and social organisation.[66] In China, the Taiping movement in the mid-nineteenth century engulfed large areas of the country. In fact it was colonialism which, far from breaking down the isolation of supposedly separate communities, did all it could to foment divisions. But it was the struggle itself that enabled these divisions to be surmounted. This is clearly illustrated in Africa where in Zimbabwe, for example, the whole basis of colonial policy was the exploitation of differences between Shona and Ndebele linguistic groups; nevertheless these two groups combined in a country-wide revolutionary movement at the end of the nineteenth century. In the Maji-maji anti-colonial war in what is today Tanzania, the leader of one community sent a message to a traditional enemy saying: "We received an order from God to the effect that all white men had to quit the country ... This war ordered by God must come first."[67]

Thus, traditional structures were not incompatible with a wider view of national and global issues. Even today, when imperialism has done much to weaken these structures, the more isolated national minority and so-called "tribal" peoples can be at the forefront of the socialist revolution—for example in the Philippines, in the Naxalbari movement in India, in Peru. In fact, the democratic trends in traditional society which have developed in opposition to local oppressors can be used as a firm foundation for a socialist and anti-imperialist movement. Cabral made a great contribution to revolutionary theory in explaining this question concretely in relation to Guinea-Bissau.[68]

None of this detracts from the fact that traditional structures would not on their own have built a new socialist mode of production without the intervention of the capitalist world system. But the whole point is the dialectics of the process whereby capitalism furthers this result. It does so not by destroying an existing stagnation, but rather by first *creating* stagnation in the place of an existing dynamism. Global capitalism has a contradictory aspect: on the one hand, the process of accumulation tends to disintegrate traditional structures, grinding them up in the process of generating surplus value, undermining them by promoting a subordinate commodity economy which forces people to abandon subsistence in favour of selling their labour and getting themselves into debt; on the other hand, the process of accumulation uses a truncated, manufactured "tradition"—the worst aspects of the old tradition, torn from the functioning system in which they used to be counterbalanced by democratic elements—in order to bolster its repressive rule. Both of these contradictory aspects contribute, in different ways, to stagnation.

The net result of the above historic logic is that the democratic struggles of the masses can no longer function as a dynamic element *within* the context of traditional society because the latter is prevented by world capitalism from developing any further along its own lines. Nor can these struggles even be harnessed as a mechanism for breaking up that society in the interests of an indigenous capitalist development which is likewise impossible; it can now only be a struggle for a complete transformation. Liberation movements carry forward what is best in the historic culture of their people in the pre-colonial era, but in a changed form. The entire world exploitative system rests on the shoulders of the masses in the colonies, and the struggles of these masses can only be struggles to overthrow this system.

NOTES

1. Marx and Engels, *The Communist Manifesto*, 45–46.

2. Lenin, *Marx-Engels-Marxism*, 67.

3. Engels, *Anti-Dühring*, 37.

4. Marx, *Oeuvres: Economie*, 1529.

5. Malthus, Volume I, Book I, Chapter VIII.

6. Ibid., 30.

7. "The necessary turning point of history is therefore the open confession, that the consciousness of God is nothing else than the consciousness of the species; that man can and should raise himself only above the limits of his individuality, and not above the laws, the positive essential conditions of his species." (Feuerbach, 270)

8. Feuerbach, 257.

9. Marx and Engels, *Selected Works*, Volume III, 358.

10. Marx and Engels, *On Colonialism*, 41.

11. While it has not been our purpose to review the literature which has appeared since the original research, we must, in

relation to the issues covered in this section, give recognition to the recent publication *Marx at the Margins: On Nationalism, Ethnicity and Non-Western Societies* by Kevin Anderson (2010). This important work of scholarship does, I believe, enrich the conclusions of our argument in this section inasmuch as—while not shying away from the issues of Eurocentrism which seem to, or actually do, exist in Marx's work—Anderson affirms Marx's immense strengths, as well as tracing a certain progressive evolution in his thinking in the direction of a greater recognition of the historicity of non-Western civilisations and the justness of their anti-colonial struggles. Anderson is to be congratulated on this. His analysis is nevertheless flawed in some respects. Lacking a grounding in the perspective of the liberation struggles, his definition of Eurocentrism is somewhat academic and superficial, resulting in a tendency sometimes to give Marx the benefit of the doubt too readily. An interesting case is the parallel he draws between the *Communist Manifesto* and Marx's writings on India. He writes, "In the *Manifesto*, Marx greeted capitalist modernization enthusiastically," (Anderson, 19) while at the same time exposing its contradictions; in a similar sense (Anderson says), Marx hailed the modernising features of colonialism in India while condemning its atrocities. This reveals quite a weak interpretation of the historical dialectic, which artificially effects a rapprochement between Marx's global analysis and his colonial analysis by undervaluing the former and overvaluing the latter. The opening of the *Manifesto* is actually much better than Anderson implies: far from enthusing about modernisation, Marx simply says that capitalism has fundamentally changed human history, and—in replacing earlier relationships by naked greed and the world market—raised for the first time the possibility of a revolution to overthrow all forms of exploitation. This argument was and remains correct (and indeed farsighted, bearing in mind that the full horrors of neo-liberalism and globalisation were merely latent in Marx's day). But in the case of India, Marx did to some extent "greet enthusiastically" aspects of colonialism's role in overcoming stagnation and the lack of private landed property. It is only by transcending this limitation that we can truly understand the historical dimension of the Indian liberation struggle, from its early anti-colonial phase right through to the present role whereby — with Marxist-Leninist-Maoist leadership at the forefront — it is bringing to fruition that very internationalist movement which the *Communist Manifesto* predicted.

12. Luxemburg, 59–60.

13. Marx and Engels, *Selected Works*, Volume II, 22.

14. Marx, *Oeuvres: Economie*, 1225 § a. (*Capital*, Volume I, Chapter XXXIII.)

15. Marx and Engels, *On Colonialism*, 313.

16. Quoted in Wood, 87.

17. Marx and Engels, *Ireland and the Irish Question*, 399–400.

18. See, for example, Rostow's *The Stages of Economic Growth: A Non-Communist Manifesto*.

19. Szentes, 24.

20. Quoted in Godelier, 50. From Marx's *Grundrisse*.

21. Marx and Engels, *Selected Works*, Volume III, 334.

22. Marx and Engels, *Selected Correspondence*, 355.

23. *Die Judenfrage als Racen-, Sitten- u, Kulturfrage*. Dühring is sometimes considered the first person to have advocated (in a later work) the extermination of the Jews.

24. Engels, *Anti-Dühring*, 14 (from the preface to the 1885 edition).

25. Ibid., 199.

26. Marx, *Oeuvres: Economie*, 368.

27. Marx and Engels, *On Colonialism*, 158.

28. Ibid., 81.

29. Ibid., 314.

30. Marx and Engels, *Selected Correspondence*, 84. Emphasis in original.

31. See Fryer, 177–179.

32. Marx and Engels, *On Colonialism*, 323.

33. Marx, *On China*, 50. This specific article was, in actual fact, written by Engels.

34. Engels, *Anti-Dühring*, Part II Chapter III.

35. Fanon, 50.

36. Engels, *Anti-Dühring*, 201.

37. Quoted in Cummins, 38.

38. Quoted in Rosdolsky, 9, 91.

39. Ibid., 170.

40. Quoted in Haupt, 16.

41. See, for example Marx, *Secret Diplomatic History of the Eighteenth Century*, 74–75.

42. James, 52–53, 80–81, 146.

43. Marx and Engels, *On Colonialism*, 319.

44. Ibid., 337–338. From Marx's letter to Meyer and Vogt (April 9, 1870).

45. Carlos Moore (b.1942) is a Black Cuban exile who has made a career out of attacking the side-lining of Black people in the Cuban revolution. Although the issue is a genuine one which needs to be taken seriously, Moore has raised it in such a way as to align himself with US imperialist attacks on Cuba,

and (as we can see in the work of Moore's which we critique here, *Were Marx and Engels White Racists?*), communism in general.

46. Marx and Engels, *Selected Correspondence*, 351, emphasis in original. From a letter to Kautsky (September 12, 1882). The deliberately distorted version of this passage is given in Moore, 38.

47. Marx and Engels, *On Colonialism*, 341, emphasis added.

48. Ibid., 320.

49. Amin, *La Loi de la valeur et le matérialisme historique*, 35–6.

50. Marx and Engels, *On Ireland*, 70.

51. Horace B. Davis's *Nationalism and Socialism* (1967) seems to tend towards such a view, but it is not very convincing.

52. Marx, *Notes on Indian History*, 40–43.

53. Ibid., 81, emphasis in original.

54. Marx, *The Ethnological Notebooks of Karl Marx*, 340.

55. Ibid., 345.

56. Ibid., 349, emphasis in original. (The last comment, which paraphrases a text of Goethe, means that Lubbock is making himself a laughing stock without realising it.)

57. See for example Marx and Engels, *On Colonialism*, 311, 314.

58. Ibid., 184 ff.

59. Ibid., 237. See also the letter of April 9, 1970, to Meyer and Vogt in Marx and Engels, *On Ireland*, 407.

60. Marx and Engels, *Selected Works*, Volume II, 404.

61. Quoted in Davis, 94.

62. Marx and Engels, *Selected Works*, Volume II, 404.

63. Marx and Engels, *On Colonialism*, 345.

64. Marx and Engels, *Selected Works*, Volume II, 404.

65. Ibid., 394.

66. See the first chapter of Sumanta Banerjee's *India's Simmering Revolution* (1984) and the sources cited.

67. Quoted in Ranger.

68. See Sigrist (1981).

The Contribution of Lenin

THE exploitative world economic system had existed since the early days of capitalism, and so had the struggle of the oppressed nations and peoples against it, but the era of imperialism marked a qualitative step. Movements of the oppressed—which become less and less isolated, and could possibly coalesce into a single current—are potentially able to move beyond the stage of simple resistance so as to actively build a new social order. This is the potential—but to realise this potential required the subjective factor, an extraordinary strategic vision, which was provided in a remarkable manner by Lenin.

There was an actual struggle of the oppressed nations and peoples for self-determination even before the political label "self-determination" was coined, and it was shaking both the Eurocentric base and superstructure of the world system. In the period leading up to the First World War colonial oppression vastly increased; during the war itself vast numbers of Asians and Africans were taken to Europe as cannon fodder or cheap substitutes for draught animals. Objectively, the world revolutionary process was becoming more and more explicitly the mission of the colonial peoples. The communist movement either had to keep up with events in its thinking or else turn into a force smothering progress.

It is in these historical circumstances that we must view the work of Lenin, a revolutionary genius whose contribution appears stronger than ever from the viewpoint which we are advocating in this book. Standing head and shoulders above most of his European contemporaries, he fully appreciated the message of the uprising of the colonial peoples. His theoretical insights and practical policies gave the communist movement an impulse which lasted—even though locked in competition with reactionary lines which later overwhelmed it—for some years. Precisely because large sections of the official movement have now completely degenerated, it is more relevant than ever to rediscover the essence of Lenin's contribution.

THEORY AND PRACTICE IN LENINISM

A great revolutionary leader is not someone born with all the answers, but someone who can learn from the mass movement; this is what Marx and Engels did with Ireland. In a sense Leninism represents a bursting forth of the real mass movement of the oppressed peoples into the ideological superstructure of communist theory. There is thus naturally an *evolution* in Lenin's thought which reflects both the evolution of the actual struggle, and the extent to which he was able to increasingly use the lessons of these struggles in order to liberate himself from Eurocentrism. This evolution can be seen if we examine three examples from Lenin's work.

The first is an article written in 1913, and aptly titled "The Historical Destiny of the Doctrine of Karl Marx." In it, Lenin analyses the characteristics of three eras in the revolutionary movement, concluding with the contemporary period which he characterises precisely by referring to the revolutionary storms in Asia:

> It is in this era of storms and their "repercussion" in Europe that we are now living. Whatever may be the fate of the great Chinese Republic, against which the various "civilised" hyenas are now gnashing their teeth,

> no power on earth can restore the old serfdom in Asia, or wipe out the heroic democracy of the masses of the people in the Asian and semi-Asian countries.[1]

This is a remarkable statement which correctly highlights the destiny of Marxism. It illustrates both the objective (the shift in geographical focus) and subjective progression of the progressive movement away from a Eurocentric focus. Lenin is describing the blowback of the struggle of the superexploited people upon the centre. However, there is still a limitation in that he tends to see the Asian movement as an extension or enlargement of a basically European pattern.[2] This limitation was progressively transcended in Lenin's later work.

Our second example comes from the period immediately after the Russian Revolution, when the Bolsheviks called a number of conferences of peoples of the East. Speaking at the second of these conferences in 1918, Lenin showed that the anticolonial movements had not only "added to" the world struggle, but also changed it qualitatively:

> It is becoming quite clear that the socialist revolution which is impending for the whole world will not be merely the victory of the proletariat of each country over its own bourgeoisie. That would be possible if revolutions came easily and swiftly. We know that the imperialists will not allow this, that all countries are armed against their domestic Bolshevism and that their one thought is how to defeat Bolshevism at home. That is why in every country a civil war is brewing in which the old socialist compromisers are enlisted on the side of the bourgeoisie. Hence **the socialist revolution will not be solely, or chiefly, a struggle of the revolutionary proletarians in each country against their bourgeoisie — no, it will be a struggle of all the imperialist-oppressed colonies and countries, of all dependent countries, against international imperialism.**[3]

The parts of this passage that we have emphasised read as an indictment of much of what has passed as "Marxist" theory in England and in many other countries up to the present day. Here, Lenin shows how the new conditions cause some of the established patterns of politics to change into their opposites. He has completely broken with unilinear views of social change. Based on their superexploitation of the rest of the world, imperialists within the core nations possess both repressive power and the ability to bribe labour leaders, the combination of which can produce a certain measure of stability that can only be disrupted by pressure at the weak point of the system. However, the *specificity* of the revolutions in the East is only partially appreciated at this stage.

Thirdly, let us consider Lenin's final work. Lenin suffered a prolonged illness before his eventual death in 1924 and could only write some short articles from his sick-bed, highlighting crucial problems of the revolution. It was precisely in this period that he returned again and again to his theme of demonstrating how, according to the dialectics of history, the cause of the world struggle was being taken up more and more by the peoples of the East, studying this theme under different angles and developing it. Faced with misguided West European radicals who claimed that "[t]he development of the productive forces of Russia has not attained the level that makes socialism possible," Lenin replied with statements such as the following:

> They have completely failed to understand what is decisive in Marxism, namely, its revolutionary dialectics. Our European philistines never even dream that the subsequent revolutions in Oriental countries, which possess much vaster populations and a much vaster diversity of social conditions, will undoubtedly display even greater distinctions than the Russian Revolution.[4]

It need hardly be said that a textbook written on Kautskyite lines was a very useful thing in its day. But it is time, for all that, to abandon the idea that it foresaw all the forms of development of subsequent world history. It would be timely to say that those who think so are simply fools.[5]

These are quite remarkable arguments. The Kautskyite "textbook" is the formalistic statement of Marxist "truths" without the revolutionary dialectics of change which is the real essence of Marxism. In contrast to his earlier "The Historical Destiny of the Doctrine of Karl Marx," Lenin sees a change in content with the new revolutions enriching Marxism through innovative forms.

On the basis of this correct worldview, Lenin also formulated practical policies stressing the importance of recognising the struggle for national self-determination, as well as targeting the close relationship between opportunism and imperialism in the metropolitan countries. These issues are still extremely relevant.

SOME LIMITATIONS IN LENINIST THEORY

Of course, Lenin's formulations also contained some limitations and weaknesses. This is quite natural; it is not materialist to expect even one of the great figures in history to arrive at an absolutely perfect position. Lenin's greatness lay in his consistent ability to move forward in resolving fresh questions, which continued right up to his death. His thought is in the same sense open-ended: he indicated a *direction* the movement as a whole needed to take in advancing and breaking fresh ground. The problem is that the official communist movement by and large failed to live up to this task.

Dialectically speaking, the weak areas which subsisted within Lenin's thought were precisely those in which a consistent application of Lenin's own standpoint and methods ought to have led his successors into making progress. This is why we are mentioning these weaknesses (or unfulfilled aspects of the progress in combating Eurocentrism) here. We will discuss some of these weaknesses in the following paragraphs.

First, although Lenin broke with Eurocentrism in practice he did not explicitly criticise or sum up the shortcomings of Marx and Engels in this respect. Secondly, closely linked with the previous point, Lenin never completely broke with the viewpoint of seeing non-European societies as historically stagnant. He did not fully understand the deep-rootedness of the forward-moving dynamic of these peoples, both in terms of the developmental thrust of traditional societies, and the sense that the anti-colonial struggle reaches back to the earliest days of capitalist expansion, carrying forward the established dynamic of these societies in a changed form. In reality, the anti-colonial movements were new to Marxism but *they were not new to history* — **they had always been there, but they simply hadn't been noticed** (from the Eurocentric frame of reference). Although they underwent a major upsurge in the era of imperialism, they did not simply spring from nowhere; however, Lenin sometimes veers towards a position of seeing these struggles as being *created* by the era of imperialism, assuming that this disrupted an earlier stagnancy. His repeated use of the adjective "new" in describing the anti-colonial movements is thus not wholly sound, although it does reflect, on the positive side, that he saw these forces as the agents of building a new era, as having unequivocally taken over the responsibility for historical progress.

This particular contradiction between the great historical vision and the surviving limitations in Lenin's worldview is well illustrated in a passage from another of his last writings where he refers, interestingly, to the orientation of a new theoretical journal. His reference to the shifting geographical focus of the world revolution as the most striking illustration of dialectics is particularly remarkable and profound:

[T]he contributors to *Pod Znamanem Marksima* must arrange for the systematic study of Hegelian dialectics from a materialist standpoint, i.e. the dialectics which Marx applied practically in his *Capital* and in his historical and political works, and applied so successfully that now every day of the awakening to life and struggle of new classes in the East (Japan, India, China)—i.e. of the hundreds of millions of human beings who form the greater part of the population of the world and whose historical passivity and historical torpor have hitherto conditioned the stagnation and decay in many advanced European countries—every day of the awakening to life of new peoples and new classes serves as a fresh confirmation of Marxism.[6]

Thirdly, Lenin was unable—essentially because of time constraints, no doubt, since he was actively leading the practical movement—to develop his work in the field of political economy. He could thus not formulate the depth of the colonial contradiction at a theoretical level to the same extent that he did in the field of practical politics.

His successors should, of course, have taken up these challenges, but did not. This was extremely unfortunate because a theoretical formulation of the broad strategic vision was absolutely necessary to counterbalance the distortions which might arise at times when the *immediate* tasks of practical politics were perhaps legitimately conceived in a somewhat Eurocentric manner.

The clearest illustration of the above problem centres around the question of inter-imperialist rivalry. In the precise circumstances of the decades leading up to World War I, the cutthroat competition between the great powers was so intense that they were driven to extend their formal, exclusive spheres of influence apparently only in order to stop their rivals doing the same. **Thus, colonial expansion appeared superficially as a function of great power rivalry.** A more correct way of presenting the question, however, would be to say that the continued existence of capitalism *as a whole* is indissolubly linked with an intensification of the superexploitation of those areas which it has made dependent. The intensification of superexploitation should not be confused *either* with an extension of the area under *formal* colonial administration *or* with rivalry over *exclusive* spheres of influence, because it can just as well take place in the absence of these two factors, as the period after World War II proves. This crucial issue was never well understood in mainstream communist theory.

When Lenin wrote *Imperialism, the Highest Stage of Capitalism*, the pressing need was to refute Kautsky's theories that imperialism could build a more stable capitalism. Kautsky was saying that the newly-formed industrial monopolies could take strategic decisions impossible under the free-competition conditions of early capitalism. The essence of Lenin's refutation of this position is that, while it is true that imperialism in some sense places on the *agenda* the rational organisation of production at the level of society as a whole (which can be carried through eventually by socialism), *it itself* is actually a parasitic and decayed form of capitalism, likely to bolster itself by extremely reactionary forms of rule in order to forestall that decay. The history of nearly a century since he wrote this book has confirmed the correctness of his prediction. Nevertheless, these correct arguments about the decayed and parasitic form — initiated around the turn of the twentieth century, and which capitalism could thereafter never escape from — should not obscure the fact that capitalism, even in its more dynamic phase, had *always* been parasitic on the natural and human resources of the periphery; or that, viewed from the South, it has always been militaristic and destructive.

Similarly, in the concrete circumstances of Lenin's time, and indeed right up to the end of World War II, the ruling classes focused enormous attention on derailing the workers' movement by propagating chauvinism against rival imperialist powers, and it became very urgent to combat this. However, it must be said that this kind of chauvinism would not have gained a foothold if it had not been for the substratum of racism, the acceptance of the right to build and maintain empires. The task of dealing with the effect of inter-imperialist rivalry was not necessarily wrong in itself, but it was extremely dangerous to conduct this task on the basis of a weak understanding of the *fundamental* contradictions, as subsequent events were to show.

NOTES

1. Lenin, *Marx-Engels-Marxism*, 78.

2. Of course, as a dialectician, Lenin realised that a change in quantity could also transform itself into a change in quality, and this is indeed how he probably saw it in this case. However, he does refer to the Asian peoples as fighting for "these same European ideals..." (ibid).

3. Lenin, *Collected Works*, Volume 30, 159, emphasis added.

4. Lenin, *Collected Works*, Volume 33, 476–480.

5. Ibid., 480.

6. Lenin, *Marx-Engels-Marxism*, 576.

The Communist Movement in the Early Twentieth Century

LENIN pointed towards the way in which the peoples of the oppressed colonial nations would become the leading force in world revolutionary progress; inevitably this meant that they would also play a leading role in the future development—not just of practical struggles but of *theory*. This inevitability, in turn, meant facing the issue of Eurocentrism squarely, and thus expanding communist theory beyond the limitations from which it still suffered.

Such a creative current did indeed begin to develop in the early years after the Russian Revolution, during which many innovative ideas were put forward. We will now briefly consider the main issues addressed at that time. In the following pages, we are not of course arguing that every one of these ideas was *correct* ... simply that the *issues* raised were genuinely important and required debate. The problem is that such challenging positions were typically only able to be advanced in spite of, or even in opposition to, the dominant ideas of the mainstream communist movement—a movement in which the spirit of Lenin's teachings was at best only partially understood. Ultimately the debate was curtailed, indeed suppressed.

The essential new ideas put forward at this time are rather difficult to state in a nutshell, but it would be helpful to pinpoint the following four questions, which are really facets of a single whole. First, the European movement must pay adequate attention and *respect* to the revolutionary movements in the colonial countries and must not marginalise them or treat them as appendages, either conceptually or in terms of practical politics and organisation. Secondly, the colonial peoples are oppressed in a qualitatively different way from the proletariat of the "advanced" countries; the former are also oppressed by capital, but the possibility of unity can only be brought about if the qualitative difference is recognised, a recognition which forms the basis of any realistic *class* analysis, or any analysis of the forces which make up the world system. Thirdly, the above divisions are reflected in a racist oppression that has *material reality*, while also being protected, at the level of ideology, by a powerful Eurocentric ideological superstructure. Fourthly, the colonial peoples must have control over their own struggles, if necessary through their own independent revolutionary organisations, this being the only basis for a genuinely united world revolutionary movement; to impose an external organisational control on these struggles is tantamount to reproducing colonial relations within the revolutionary movement itself.

The above four ideas are among the most important revolutionary concepts of twentieth century world history. The fact that they were in many cases put forward by Third World Marxists is proof that Marxism is the most revolutionary ideology, and confirmation of the genius of Lenin; the fact that these ideas have often been elbowed out of the official communist movement is proof that the strength of Eurocentrism must not be underestimated.

THE CRISIS AFTER WORLD WAR I:
"TACTICAL EUROCENTRISM"

The period immediately after World War I and the Russian Revolution was one of acute crisis for capitalism—of this both imperialists and revolutionaries had no doubt. Some thought that this heralded a final apocalyptic downfall of the system. Lenin probably did not make this mistake, and accepted the *possibility* of the system consolidating itself to some degree; what he argued, correctly, is that imperialism is an era which constantly raises also the possibility of revolutions. Whatever further developments capitalism undergoes cannot fundamentally alleviate, but can only intensify, the misery and exploitation of the working masses (as we see all too clearly today with "globalisation"). Furthermore, because of its spatial and temporal *unevenness* (temporally, periodic crisis and, spatially, the existence of weak links and the rivalry between rising and declining imperialist powers), there exists the possibility of revolution at particular times and places: it is the duty of revolutionaries to "seize the time."

This is a perspective that will apply throughout the era of imperialism, particularly at times when one of its major structural phases has entered its crisis—an example is the situation in the late 1960s and 1970s. At this point in our analysis, though, we will focus on the situation right after World War I: the social order in Europe was gravely shaken, while the ruling class frantically sought to overthrow the Russian Revolution to prevent it from giving further encouragement to social radicals. In these circumstances, it would not be surprising to find the emergence of a phenomenon which we might describe as "tactical Eurocentrism," whereby Europe would appear as the *immediate* focus of world events. Despite the fact that Lenin was, as we have seen, arguing precisely the opposite in a strategic sense, such a tactical Eurocentrism appears on the surface quite reasonable, and was to appear even more so in the subsequent period, first with the rise of Hitler and then, after World War II, in response to aggressive imperialist policies like the Cold War and the formation of NATO. However, from its origin, this position carried with it severe dangers, as can be seen in the text of the Manifesto of the First Congress of the (Third) Communist International, drafted by Trotsky:

> The workers and peasants not only of Annam, Algiers and Bengal, but also of Persia and Armenia will gain their opportunity of independent existence only in that hour when the workers of England and France, having overthrown Lloyd George and Clemenceau, will have taken state power into their own hands. Colonial slaves of Africa and Asia! The hour of proletarian dictatorship in Europe will strike for you as the hour of your own emancipation![1]

There is a clear indication, here, that the revolution in the East is subordinate, both in essence and politically, to the revolution of the advanced capitalist countries. It is interesting to note, in this context, that Trotsky also assumes that "smaller peoples" can freely exist only because the proletarian revolution will "free the productive forces of all countries from the tentacles of the national states," and calls upon them to direct their affairs "without any detriment to the unified and centralised European and world economy."[2] Such an argument—which is tantamount to saying that the post-revolutionary world economy will be run from Europe and colonial peoples must do nothing to rock the boat—is an extreme projection of Eurocentrism: it wholly differs from Lenin's stance that, while the example of Soviet Russia could create favourable conditions for revolution in the East, the latter could then proceed with its own independent momentum, a relationship which in no way implies subordination.

In the early period after the Russian Revolution, there were powerful currents opposing this political Eurocentrism which helped hold its dangers in check. The dialectic between these opposing forces can be understood in the context of an important debate about the nature of the revolution in the colonial world and its relationship with Russia. We can see this in the report on the national and colonial question delivered by the Soviet representative Pavlovitch at the Baku conference of the Peoples of the East (1920). Here he employs a curious mixed metaphor: "If into this compound [i.e. the East] which is densely saturated with the revolutionary bacteria we introduce a crystal in the form of peasant soviets, soviets of the toilers, the resulting crystallisation will proceed with rapid strides."[3]

The chemistry may be dodgy, but the general idea is clear; it is preferable to Trotsky's stance but still contains certain weaknesses. First, as Lenin was to recognise, the national movements should be able to develop their own forms of social organisation, and secondly the condition for a direct development to socialism, bypassing the stage of capitalism, is not only the existence of the Russian Revolution as an example, but also the blocked or dependent character of domestic capitalist development in the colonial or neo-colonial countries. Nevertheless, it was generally healthy and progressive that the movement was debating these issues. The worst thing is to stifle the debate: by seeking to prevent "wrong" ideas being debated you are more likely to consolidate a reactionary dogma and make it immune to critique.

The theory of the East being able to skip the capitalist stage is extremely interesting because it can be found in the context of arguments coming from radically different positions. In Lenin's case, it arose on the basis of a profound sense that the geographical focus of social innovation was shifting away from the Eurocentric area into which capitalism had temporarily and artificially corralled it—precisely because of its great revolutionary potential, the East can develop great creativity in finding historically new paths to social change. But the position of saying that the East can skip the capitalist stage was also compatible with a diametrically opposite view which marginalised the actually existing struggles, making the "skipping" conditional upon accepting the leadership of the colonizing countries under a proletarian guise.

This is not to say that all the struggles, which occurred during the period when debate was still flourishing, are ones that we can really consider constructive in the sense of pushing the theory forward. We also find something which I will call "phoney line-struggles": since Eurocentrism could occur under a number of different guises, which superficially appear to be in contradiction with one another, we find the phenomenon of phoney line-struggles which, in reality, merely pit one form of Eurocentrism against another, each of them proceeding from the same fundamental premises. The line at the Baku conference was an extremely leftist form of this line; it tended to repudiate those national movements which lacked an explicit revolutionary orientation, and even went so far as to justify the English working class's indifference to the Irish struggle on the grounds that

> suppose the Irish separatists succeed in their aim and realise their cherished ideal of an independent Irish people. The very next day, independent Ireland would fall under the yoke of American capital or of the French Bourse, and, perhaps within a year or two Ireland would be fighting against Britain or some other states in alliance with one of the world predators, for markets, for coal mines, for iron mines, for bits of territory in Africa.[4]

The above quotation is an example of the reactionary conclusions that can result from an ultra-left premise; here the speaker assumes that the skipping of capitalism can only be in the direction of "pure" (soviet) socialism and hence writes off all the real, concrete conditions of the revolutions in colonial countries. At the same time, however, there is also a more obviously rightist position which can be derived from the idea of skipping the capitalist stage: this is the set of ideas which were to receive systematic form in the subsequent Soviet theory known as that of the "non-capitalist road of development."

"LEFT" AND RIGHT MARGINALISATION OF THIRD WORLD STRUGGLES

The latter theory—which matured in the post-World War II Soviet Union, but on a basis of earlier Eurocentric lines—implies that colonial countries are backward, with poorly-formed class relations, but that if they stick closely to the Soviet Union their political development will witness the emergence of progressively-inclined regimes, lacking a clear class character, but which tend to lay the groundwork for socialism. This reasoning can be traced to the concept of history-less peoples incapable of generating their own dynamic class relations, and therefore awaiting the kiss of life from outside. Such a line converts the marginalisation of the colonial peoples in the ideological sphere into an actual blueprint for their physical, political, and economic marginalisation within the Soviet sphere.

During the heyday of the "non-capitalist road" theory (in the 1970s and early '80s), whenever Soviet historians looked back at the Comintern period they tended to home in on those aspects which anticipated their own social-imperialist line.[5] They are partially correct because that reactionary line was indeed anticipated by *part* of what was being said in the Comintern, but it is an over-simplification—there were real debates. In some respects, these debates tended to be conducted on shared Eurocentric premises, between "left" and right ways of marginalising the colonial struggles, i.e. between, on the one hand, seeing them as purely proletarian and devoid of significant national character, and on the other, pinning too much faith on a particular faction of the bourgeoisie.

This does not, however, encompass the whole political topography of the Comintern period. There were also beneficial and progressive debates about real issues. Thus we find, superimposed on the debate we have just described, another that started from different premises, i.e. a debate which accepted the intrinsic strategic importance of the struggles in the colonial world. It is to this debate that we must now turn because it contains lessons, which will be instructive in today's anti-Eurocentric struggle. The trends, which developed on a basis of these more correct premises, included not only the ideas of Lenin, which we have already mentioned, but also those held by a number of leading revolutionaries from the oppressed nations.

The Second Congress of the Communist International in 1920 witnessed a fairly intense debate between Lenin and the Indian communist, M.N. Roy. The crux of the dispute, according to Roy's later recollection, was the assessment of the objective role of the Indian nationalist leader, Gandhi.[6] Lenin considered Gandhi progressive in terms of the anti-imperialist struggle at that time whereas Roy thought his role should be assessed primarily in social terms, hence it was reactionary. This debate is a good example of a "contradiction among the people" which is helpful in advancing the theory and practice of the movement, and the issues raised remain important to the present day. Lenin's position obviously has nothing in common with the theory of the "non-capitalist road"—he is not saying that the movement led by Gandhi could build a kind of dependent "socialism" under Soviet patronage. Roy, for his part, held a very correct position on political economy that placed the question of colonial exploitation at the centre of the picture: "Super-profit gained in the colonies is the mainstay of modern capitalism, and so long as the latter is not deprived of this source of super-profit, it will not be easy for the European working class to overthrow the capitalist order."[7]

Roy made an incorrect deduction from these correct premises by assuming that if the colonies are basic to the political economy of capitalism, this can only be because capitalism is breaking up the existing relations of production and spreading capitalistic ones; hence he overestimated the class character of the struggle in the peripheries. It was only much later, with the formulation of the theories about the centre-periphery relationship and unequal development that it has been possible to arrive at a properly dialectical position on this question. The fact is that capitalism realises its super-profit not *only* by disintegrating traditional structures, but by *maintaining*, within the context of a world economy overwhelmingly dominated by the capitalism of the big powers, a certain non-capitalist sector in the colonial and neo-colonial countries, thus allowing part of the articles of subsistence and maintenance of the labourer to be assured outside the capitalist sector. On this basis, labour power can be obtained below its value; the development of fully-fledged capitalist relations of production is thus blocked—this is one reason why central capitalism exploits both classes and nations.

STRUGGLES OVER THE COLONIAL QUESTION: "PROLETARIANISED NATIONS"

Such a dialectical perspective could only be arrived at as a result of an intensive process of debate between people who shared a common premise of validating the movements of the South, but who held conflicting or partially correct ideas about the significance of particular trends. Such a debate did exist in the early years after the Russian Revolution, only to be stifled soon after—which is why it was to take another half century before dependency theory could eventually address some of these issues. Roy was only one of those who argued persistently against the marginalisation of the colonial question.[8] Pak Din Shun, the Korean delegate to the Second Comintern Congress in 1920, who seems to have taken a centrist position in the early debates over the emphasis on class and national struggle, wrote a critique of the past history of the European labour movement's line on the colonial question, criticising the manner in which the question had been dealt with at the First Comintern Congress; the Second Congress, he argued, "should direct its attention to the East where the fate of the world revolution may be decided."[9]

Perhaps the most interesting figure who contributed to this brief debate was Sultan Galiev—a Muslim from one of the nations oppressed within the old Russian Empire—who played a leading role in the early period of the Soviet revolution. His importance lies in the fact that, by pushing the argument to extreme (but not necessarily correct) conclusions, he posed the issues with an exceptional clarity. He is the figure which the latter-day Soviet authorities found most frightening: a 1979-published official Soviet compilation on the Comintern and the East[10] did not even mention his name, which is an astonishing distortion of history considering that in any objective study of this subject he would necessarily figure as one of the central characters.[11] The Soviet leaders of the 1970s could just about, gingerly, bring themselves to touch Roy, but the issues raised by Sultan Galiev were so explosive that it was safer to sweep them under the carpet, even 60 years later.

Galiev's starting point was that communism had made a grave strategic mistake "in devoting prior attention to the revolutionary movement in Western Europe, forgetting that the weak point of the capitalist world is in the Orient, not the Occident."[12] But the conclusions that he drew from this premise were sharply different from those of Roy. On the same premise as Roy—that the superexploitation of the colonies was the factor underpinning the capitalist system—Sultan Galiev drew the opposite conclusion, namely that they are exploited as nations and thus become, in essence, *proletarian nations*. In 1918, one of Galiev's followers argued that the oppressed nations can be regarded as "proletarian peoples, for they are the only people genuinely oppressed. They are more authentically proletarian than are the English or French proletariat."[13]

The above claim amounts to saying that, if these peoples are the most authentically revolutionary force, they must be paid the respect of allowing local communists to take account of local conditions, and form class alliances on that basis. Moreover, a change in power from bourgeoisie to proletariat in the industrialised countries could not in reality remove national oppression (as was often assumed)—only an *independent* movement of the colonial and semi-colonial countries could achieve this. The organisational conclusion, for Sultan Galiev, was to advocate the creation of a special international communist organisation of Asiatic and colonial peoples.

ORGANISATIONAL CONCLUSIONS OF THE THIRD WORLD MARXISTS

A strikingly similar view to Sultan Galiev's conception of proletarian nations was put forward (almost certainly independently of Galiev himself) by Li Dazhao, the founder of Marxism in China. Writing in January 1920, Li Dazhao expressed the view that China as a whole had been proletarianised with respect to the world system.[14] Note that this thesis in no way led Li to deny the importance of class struggle or the need for communist leadership in China; the point was to achieve a new, more accurate formulation of the central issue in world politics, precisely for the purpose of bringing Marxist analysis and communist leadership to bear upon it. In 1924 Li went further and highlighted Eurocentrism in an explicit and farsighted way, stating that there is a racial issue in world politics and the responsibility for introducing this lay with "the world view of the Europeans [for whom] there is nothing else to speak of except Christianity, and as far as their world view is concerned, they think that there is only the white man's world."[15] They see themselves "as pioneers of culture in the world, they place themselves in a superior position and look down on other races as inferior. Because of this the race question has become a class question and the races, on a world scale, have come to confront each other as classes."[16] Bearing in mind the left's historic denial of racism, this is a truly remarkable statement.

On the basis of such a worldview, very specific and crucial questions of strategy and organisation are implied. These were addressed, also around the same period, by an African communist, Lamine Senghor. Senghor was working in France and had difficulties with the French Communist Party due to his advocacy of independent Black organisations. He accepted the need for an inter-colonial union as part of the communist movement, but insisted that independent of this there must be built something which, in his words, "is not a movement of charlatans run by a white politician with humanitarian views, but a universal movement destined to uphold the rights, interests and prestige of the Black Race."[17] This plan took shape in the Comité de Défense de la Race Nègre (Committee in Defence of the Negro Race) founded in 1928 by Senghor and Gourang Kouyate. It must be stressed that it was not the intention to liquidate communist leadership: the point was that Marcus Garvey had recently revealed the enormous storm which could be unleashed by a mass mobilisation of Black people no longer prepared to live under racism, and Lamine Senghor had sensed the revolutionary potential of bringing this under the guidance of a non-Eurocentric communist worldview. Unfortunately, Senghor died the following year, but already his initiative had met with a frosty response from the authorities within the communist movement.

We have mentioned briefly a number of ideas, which emerged from communists mainly from the colonial world in the period immediately after the Russian Revolution. Hopefully we have shown that this reflects the real existence, and potential, of a trend to push the debate into new areas, and eventually expand the horizons of communism to make it become, under the leadership of non-European communists themselves, a revolutionary theory which is truly the property of humanity as a whole. Issues raised in this great debate remain as lively and relevant as they were then: they are a testament to the vitality and relevance of the movement and have never disappeared. But the chance for these issues to have an *immediate* impact on organised communism, presented by these great debates of the 1920s, was tragically stifled and crushed soon after. This resulted in tremendous setbacks and missed opportunities.

NOTES

1. *Theses, Resolutions and Manifestos of the First Four Congresses of the Third International*, 32.

2. Ibid., 31

3. *Baku: Congress of the Peoples of the East*, 100.

4. Ibid., 102.

5. See Ulyanovsky's edited collection *The Comintern and the East* (1979), particularly Persits's article, "Eastern Internationalists in Russia and some Questions of the National Liberation Movement (1918–July 1920)."

6. Ibid., 424.

7. Quoted in Bashear, 14.

8. He also made a strong attack on this issue at the Third Congress of the Comintern in 1921.

9. Quoted in Bashear, 13. From an article in *the Communist International* (June–July 1920).

10. See Ulyanovsky (1979).

11. He was, during the early period and among other things, Stalin's assistant in the People's Commisariat for Nationalities, and editor of its paper, *Zhizn Natsionalnosty*.

12. Quoted in Bennigson, 404.

13. Quoted in Bennigson, 401.

14. Quoted in Meisner, 401.

15. Quoted in Meisner, 190–191.

16. Ibid.

17. Front culturel sénégalais, 14.

Between Lenin And Mao: The Comintern Period

THE smothering of debate on the strategy for colonial struggles was linked in an interesting way to Soviet policy towards the non-Russian nationalities within the old Russian Empire. Lenin had foreseen the importance of this question: alongside his general characterisation of the era, discussed above, he had reflected on the concrete issues upon which the movement must take a stance. In this context, a particular danger for communist parties in the metropolitan countries was compromise with, or even espousal of, their "own" nation's colonialism. As well as waging an important struggle against this danger in West European parties, Lenin did the same in his own country, fighting a deathbed struggle against Great Russian chauvinism. In one of his dictated notes, dated December 31, 1922, Lenin wrote:

> It would be unpardonable opportunism if, on the eve of the debut of the East, just as it is awakening, we undermined our prestige with its peoples, even if only by the slightest crudity or injustice towards our own non-Russian nationalities. The need to rally against the imperialists of the West, who are defending the capitalist world, is one thing. There can be no doubt about that, and it would be superfluous for me to speak about my unconditional approval of it. It is another thing when

we ourselves lapse into imperialist attitudes towards oppressed nationalities, even if only in trifles, thus undermining all our principled sincerity, all our principled defence of the struggle against imperialism. But the morrow of world history will be a day when the awakening peoples oppressed by imperialism are finally aroused and the decisive long and hard struggle for their liberation begins.[1]

But this warning was not heeded. At the Twelfth Congress of the Russian Communist Party (Bolsheviks) in 1923 a resolution was passed which treats small-nation nationalism on a par with Great Russian chauvinism, condemning both equally. Such a position, which is very close to what was later reproduced by the Communist Party of China, is wrong in principle, because it puts the oppressor and oppressed on par. Shortly after the adoption of that position, Sultan Galiev was placed under arrest.[2]

With Lenin's disappearance from the scene, the debate quickly came to an end, and simultaneously a Eurocentric approach to the assessment of the focus of contradictions became an ingrained habit. In this sense, the communist movement missed its rendezvous with history, with the great challenges of the twentieth century. In respect to the fairly short period of real debate we have just described, it should again be emphasised that we are not saying all the ideas put forward by these particular figures were necessarily correct, but we are most definitely saying that they were raising the correct issues: the question was whether the communist movement could be brought into contact with the essence of the struggles of most of the oppressed peoples, instead of making a futile attempt to impose itself upon them in a formal and external way. The price for failure in this historic task was to be the dissipation of the potential of oppressed-nation struggles into trends like Nasserism and Sukarnoism. Of course, non-communist national movements, and any other struggles, which oppose imperialism at a particular time, may in certain circumstances be progressive and worthy of support. But it is only the integration of the national movements with Marxism-Leninism that can fundamentally change the conditions of the oppressed peoples in the long term.

"KAUTSKYITE" ANALYSIS OF IMPERIALISM: PHONEY TWO-LINE STRUGGLE

After Lenin's death the overwhelming tendency in the international communist movement was for one aspect of the era of imperialism (the tendency for the formation of monopolies, for the dominance of finance capital, etc.) to be enshrined in lifeless textbooks, written, in Lenin's phrase, "on Kautskyite lines,"[3] and arbitrarily carved away from the other aspect with which it should be dialectically linked, namely the intensified exploitation *and resistance* of the peoples of the oppressed nations. Of course, acute struggles continued within the Soviet leadership after Lenin's death, but they tended to sidestep the real issues and be conducted on the basis of shared Eurocentric premises.

At first sight, this seems strange because one of the main targets of these struggles was the ideas of Trotsky, and Trotsky's position was generally Eurocentric: he tended to downplay the revolutionary potential of the peasantry and of the national question, and on this basis to consider the prolongation of the Russian Revolution to be logically in the direction of the West rather than the East. Moreover, the ultimate victor in the post-Lenin leadership struggle was actually the person who, in terms of his political background, had been comparatively strong in backing Lenin's fight *against* the Eurocentric trend—Stalin. In order to understand this seeming paradox, we will briefly analyse Stalin's role.

In 1918 when, as he put it, "the eyes of all are naturally turned to the West," Stalin wrote an article entitled "Don't Forget the East." In the historical circumstances of the time, that statement was certainly progressive. Nevertheless, there were errors in the way he conceived this stance, the significance of which would become clear later. Notably, Stalin's formulations were quite mechanical:

> It is the task of communism to break the age-long sleep of the oppressed peoples of the East, to infect the workers and peasants of these countries with the emancipatory spirit of revolution, to rouse them to fight imperialism, and thus deprive world imperialism of its "most reliable" rear and "inexhaustible" reserve.[4]

This statement lacks the sense, present even in Lenin's least satisfactory formulations, of the oppressed nations *creatively* taking up the banner of the world communist movement. And subsequently, despite being acclaimed as a theoretician on the national question, Stalin developed some very strange positions on this question. For example, in one of his more theoretically inclined works, Stalin astonishingly argues that national oppression is essentially the fault of the landed aristocracy—with the result that it tends to *grow weaker* as development proceeds along the lines of capitalism, and the bourgeoisie progressively elbow landowners aside. Thus, in the case of England, where the landed aristocracy have been forced to share power with the bourgeoisie, "national oppression is milder, less inhuman—if, of course, we disregard the fact that in the course of this war, when power has passed into the hands of the landlords, national oppression has become much more severe (persecution of the Irish, Indians)." This presents a very weird and unrecognisable picture of British imperialism. Even worse: in countries like Switzerland and North America, Stalin continues, where only the bourgeoisie hold power and there are no landlords, "the nationalities develop more or less freely, and, generally speaking, there is practically no soil for national oppression."[5]

Most strikingly, Stalin here apparently fails to perceive how the genocide and oppression of Native Americans and Black slaves has underpinned the whole of North American nation-building. But in a wider sense, he seems quite unaware of the fundamental role played by national oppression within both the base and superstructure of the capitalist mode of production in general, and of its imperialist phase in particular. These arguments, enshrined in the official Moscow edition of Stalin's *Works*, must rank among the worst, and perhaps the most eccentric, in the history of Eurocentrism. Therefore, it is not surprising that the lines of demarcation in Soviet inner-party struggles were incorrectly drawn.

POLITICAL ECONOMY IN THE PERIOD OF THE COMINTERN

The weaknesses of the overall worldview of the communist movement in the inter-war period are particularly revealed in the field of political economy, which can be considered the most systematic expression of this worldview. An interesting example is A. Leontiev's textbook *Political Economy*, which constituted the established orthodoxy for international communism in the 1930s. It is difficult to categorise Leontiev's procedure (which, it should be noted, received official blessing) other than as a falsification of Lenin. Thus, when Leontiev gives the party line in attacking Bukharin and other opposition elements, he lists the contradictions which become intensified under imperialism, and which Bukharin allegedly neglects. But Leontiev's list completely marginalises the colonial question: "the contradiction between the bourgeoisie and the proletariat, the struggle within the capitalist camp, anarchy of production, crises."[6] To justify this one-sided image, he quotes Lenin as follows: "[i]mperialism emerged as the development and direct continuation of the fundamental attributes of capitalism in general."[7] And yet this truncated quote grossly distorts Lenin's intended meaning. If we turn to the original, we see that Lenin continues as follows:

> But capitalism only became capitalist imperialism at a very definite and very high stage of its development, when certain of its fundamental characteristics began to change into their opposites, when the features of the epoch of transition from capitalism to a higher social and economic system had taken shape and revealed themselves all along the line.[8]

From what we have already discussed, it is obvious that Lenin meant this fundamental change centrally to include the rising up of the world's people, particularly the peoples oppressed by imperialism—this is precisely what is meant by the transition to a new system. In fact, in line with our earlier argument, Lenin's position was not wholly correct, inasmuch as his attribution of "newness" to the struggles of the East underplays the role that colonial exploitation, and the struggles against it, had *always* played within the capitalist base and superstructure. Nevertheless, Lenin is right that this is the first time when a new order in the interests of the oppressed could actually be constructed. We can be categorical that any attempt to invoke Lenin to justify a vision of the imperialist epoch shorn of national exploitation and struggle is a blatant falsification.

In line with his reactionary worldview, Leontiev therefore retrenches himself in a sterile and useless picture of imperialism as simply an extension or intensification of some definition of a capitalist system which itself lacks any sense of reality. Indeed, incredibly, he devotes less than one page (out of 282 in the English edition) to discussing the enslavement of the colonies! Clearly, for him, this is the most peripheral subject imaginable. Leontiev's work is the epitome of exactly the kind of "lifeless textbook" which Lenin warned against.

The Soviet position after Lenin therefore took as its starting-point a departure from dialectics, in this case a wooden and one-sided treatment of capitalism and its imperialist era. And, as Lenin said:

Any fragment, segment, section of this curve (of human knowledge) can be transformed (transformed one-sidedly) into an independent, complete, straight line, which then (if one does not see the wood for the trees) leads into the quagmire, into clerical obscurantism (where it is *anchored* by the class interests of the ruling classes).[9]

Of course, given the dominant role of the Soviet party, the whole international movement in turn became infected by this undialectical one-sidedness, and by the reactionary conclusions to which it led.

But our argument here is that, although we should recognise the factor of Soviet influence, this excuse is not sufficient to get the European communist parties off the hook for their Eurocentrism. Reactionary lines on the colonial question unquestionably found an independent source within the imperialist countries and it is within these countries that, arguably, these political lines first became anchored in the interests of the ruling classes. If, in some respects, the downgrading of the colonial question could, in the Soviet Union, initially be regarded as an *error* (even though from the beginning it also had an aspect of Great Russian chauvinism, of which Lenin was acutely aware), then in the imperialist countries this problem objectively signified an apology for their "own" colonialism, which is even worse. Thus, when the Communist Party of Great Britain published its own "Marxist Study Courses" on Political Economy (1932–3) it even outdid Leontiev by devoting only one paragraph (in the middle of p. 522) out of a total length of 548 pages to a direct assessment of colonialism. We may note that this book is marked throughout its length by an apoplectic fever-pitch of a polemic against Trotskyism and social democracy (characteristic of the "left" phase of the CPGB), yet nowhere are the lines of demarcation correctly drawn. Trotsky's theory of imperialism is thus attacked on the grounds that "[h]e completely ignores capitalist monopolies. As far as he is concerned finance capital is identical with loan capital. The struggle to partition the world is depicted by Trotsky as a struggle merely for markets where to unload commodities."[10] And the rest of the critique continues in a similar vein. One might have thought that a 548 page book attacking Trotsky would provide a good context to address the line on the national question and peasantry, but this is precisely what does not happen. These themes are simply censored from the realm of political economy. We must, therefore, conclude that the contradiction with Trotsky was to a considerable extent, in its actual form, a phoney two-line struggle.

The theory developed by the Communist International (Comintern) thus effectively imposed a conceptual straitjacket on attempts at creative political thought. Its fundamental failure of analysis was its refusal to recognise the relationship between capitalism and imperialism and the colonies as the essential basis for accumulation and the division of labour. On this corrupt basis it is not surprising that disastrous political errors occurred.

When the capitalist world economy entered a period of intense crisis at the end of the 1920s and during the '30s, the Comintern put forward a theory of "general crisis" which asserted that there was no escape for capitalism.[11] This did not allow for the possibility that a global capitalist system, which had always been fundamentally premised on the superexploitation of the South, could restructure itself—in a sense even revitalise its exploitative potential—precisely through an intensification of that exploitation. Clinging obstinately to its erroneous view, it was inevitable that the Soviet-led communist movement would sooner or later fall into an ideological trap of its own making, and become imprisoned therein. This is exactly what happened after 1945, a period that witnessed, on the one hand, a considerable recovery and expansion of capitalism and, on the other (its essential foundation), an intensified exploitation of the South, leading to potentially unprecedented forces of resistance. But to the Soviet party of the time, this structural development came as too much of a shock. In order to look at these developments squarely in the face it would have to recognise that the foundations of its previous worldview, notably in the late 1920s and '30s, were flawed. If one could only recognise that the exploitation of the South had *always* been the foundation of capitalism/imperialism (and the liberation movements its Achilles heel), then the postwar boom and neo-colonialism would stand out as a huge confirmation of the correctness of Marxism-Leninism. But, wedded to its wrong ideology, the official movement was left with only one response—denial! It therefore continued to stick, in the postwar period, to its general crisis theory against all the evidence, refused to recognise either the exploitation or the potential for resistance, and departed further and further from the Marxist method of seeking truth from facts as it had earlier abandoned revolutionary dialectics. Instead of being the most unflinching portrayal of reality, Soviet Marxism became distorted, fabricated, and threadbare; it is not surprising, then, that this system itself, clutching its illusions, eventually went to its doom.

THE DEAD HAND OF ORTHODOXY: THE CASE OF PALME DUTT

It seems that, once the wave of creative Marxism had been dispersed after the early '20s, a kind of dead hand descended, effectively limiting any promise of new developments. To illustrate this deadening, we can consider the trajectory of one of the leading figures in the European movement—Rajani Palme Dutt of the Communist Party of Great Britain. It is worth noting that Dutt, himself descended from one of the oppressed colonial nations, quickly became the Party's leading theoretician;[12] this development appeared as if to have the potential to be part of the tide of self-assertion by communists of the oppressed nations (of which we have noted several cases) but he was eventually reduced to toeing the line.

One indeed discerns some promising tendencies that were sadly soon nipped in the bud. Dutt's book, *World Politics 1918–36* (written in 1936), while not ascending to the level of comprehending accumulation on a world scale, does make a considerable contribution in anticipating the concept of unequal exchange, which was to become one of the important aspects of the creative trend in Marxism subsequently developed in the 1970s. He writes:

> The essence of the relations of the colonies and imperialism is inequality. The colonial peoples are compelled by a whole series of devices and regulations, depriving them of their land, hut taxes, poll taxes, etc. to labour and produce the raw materials for prices which leave them on a starvation level. The prices of the goods which are exported to the colonies are on a high level. It is unequal exchange, which is in fact maintained by armed force, and which yields the high colonial super-profits to the capitalists of the ruling country. To this unequal exchange is added the direct tribute on the export of capital.[13]

This analysis possesses potential, and recalls the farsighted "drain" theory put forward around 1900 by another eminent Indian scholar, Dadabhai Naoroji. Nevertheless, the underlying weakness in Dutt's vision is that exploitation is seen as a bad thing, but not as characteristic of the system. While he perceived superexploitation at an empirical level, Dutt was prevented by the general climate of Eurocentrism from drawing the necessary conclusions. In particular, in *World Politics 1918–36*, he wrongly argues that *sovereign rule* by the colonial power is "the pivot of the whole complex,"[14] thereby failing to register that the fundamental socio-economic "drain" relationship can exist largely independent of whether a country is a formal colony or not. In this way his thought slips into a sterile byway, where the exploitative relationship is seen as being entirely reproduced by force (even though this view had effectively been debunked by Engels in his examination of the "force theory" in *Anti-Dühring*) and is blocked and imprisoned there. This weakness possibly underlies Dutt's postwar degeneration into an apologist of some of the most reactionary Soviet positions. Thus, by the early '60s, when formal colonialism was on the wane, Dutt heavily insisted on the fact that in 1963 only 1.7% of the world's population was under direct colonial rule, thus parroting the then Soviet leadership's assertions that, since colonialism was no longer an issue,[15] the world system was shifting (under Soviet influence) in a fundamentally progressive direction. Such a stance of course underplays the key importance of *neo*-colonialism, whereby the powers can maintain domination, perhaps more efficiently, through relinquishing formal sovereignty. In fact, indirect forms of rule were already being experimented with in wide areas of the South in the 1930s — at the time when Dutt wrote his 1936 book — for example, in Latin America and the Middle East. After World War II, with the decolonisation process, such indirect forms of rule were generalised to most of the world system where they formed a reliable basis for precisely the kind of intensified superexploitation that enabled capitalism to restructure itself.

The mechanism which forced Dutt to block off his more creative streak, and ultimately turn into a leading exponent of the dead hand of orthodoxy, was the Eurocentric *global view* which he was expected to believe, even though it stood in contradiction with some of his better insights. In Dutt's 1936 book we can already see the effect of certain tenets which the dominant perspective made it impossible for him to question. Thus, with pure orthodoxy, he discusses the colonial question mainly from the viewpoint of a redistribution among the great powers, rather than that of an accentuated exploitation from which they would all benefit **and which they might eventually (in the postwar phase of multilateral imperialism) learn collectively to manage.** Dutt argues that what might in 1913 have appeared as a world system advancing "to ever closer world interdependence and interrelationships" had now been revealed as one "with centrifugal tendencies of break-up of closer world relations towards a system of restricted world trade, separate and competing financial bases of unstably related currencies, weakened international division of labour, and intensified warfare of the monopolist blocs."[16]

The view expressed here, in line with Comintern general crisis theory, is an extremely mechanistic and unilinear vision of imperialism, which implies that the system will crassly stumble into its own grave. It fails to penetrate the hidden reality of world politics which, in what one might effectively consider a condominium of the great powers over the oppressed nations, served as a prerequisite for their squabbles over the spoils. Of course, the sphere of great power contention and contradictions has always been, and remains, an extremely important subject of analysis. But Dutt's infatuation with the splitting apart of international relations during the '30s (protectionism, tariff barriers, declining trade between the powers) is tantamount to saying that the *whole content* of international economic and political relations is the relations between great powers, a classic symptom of Eurocentrism. Moreover, it neglects many concrete facts of great importance. Even the splitting apart of international relations in the 1930s was explicitly and deliberately linked with closer *integration* between the metropoles and their respective spheres of influence, i.e. it was fundamentally premised upon increased superexploitation of the colonies. From a non-Eurocentric analysis, we should say that the international division of labour thus continued unabated through the world economic crisis. The only peculiarity of the period prior to the end of World War II is that there was temporarily an increased stress on the exclusive exploitation of colonies by *particular* imperialist powers.

The crisis of the '30s was a period of unparalleled misery for the colonies, but not because they were less involved in the international division of labour; on the contrary they suffered all of its ill-effects. For example, the tendency of the forcible conversion of colonies to cash-crop production went on apace; as Walter Rodney has shown, profits from this source actually increased during the Depression.[17] Such an accentuated enslavement, initially conducted under a colonial *command* economy, would later be inherited by a world *market* economy and jointly imposed by the capitalist core upon the South. The grave error of general crisis theory was to present a kind of unilinear vision whereby, once some trend dangerous to international capitalism (such as the collapse of world trade) had been initiated, it could never be reversed. In reality, even though it is true that imperialism signalled some sort of transition into a stage of decay of the capitalist mode of production, there was still scope for the readjustment of many of its specific features. Capitalism could very well adapt to secure for itself, under multilateral auspices, a phase of increased world trade—as indeed occurred, first after 1945 and then later with the creation of the WTO which used this increased trade precisely as a vehicle for an intensified exploitative international division of labour.

Given these fundamental weaknesses in the overall parameters of the official worldview within which they were obliged to operate, it is hardly surprising that individual communists like Dutt, far from updating their theories to encompass new realities, would become mired in a cesspit of denial and theoretical regression.

ASSESSMENT OF THE COMINTERN

During the period of its existence, the Third International (Comintern) functioned as a kind of headquarters of the world communist movement, discussing global ideological trends and formulating a common strategy. Although there are some dangers in this—it may make it more difficult for radicals in a particular country to come to grips with their own concrete reality—the aspiration for a common political and theoretical line, a common strategy and tactics, against imperialism possesses a certain logic (it should give us cause for reflection that by the time imperialism had developed its own increasingly coordinated strategy—through NATO, OECD, etc.—after World War II, the Comintern had ceased to exist). We therefore in no way minimise the noble causes which were fought for under the banner of the Comintern. The problem was not the existence of a common line per se but the *content* of that line: the Eurocentric basis on which it was determined, a deep-seated tendency to subordinate anti-colonial struggles to a strategy worked out essentially in the industrial heartlands, and as a function of issues in those heartlands.

Concretely, this weakness was embodied in two more or less parallel tendencies, which were mutually reinforcing. One was the Eurocentrism of Soviet foreign policy and its reflection in the analyses of the Comintern, increasingly closely tied to the foreign policy of the Soviet *state*; the other was the growing social-colonialist line within Western European communist parties.

During the period of the growth of fascism in Europe from the beginning of the 1930s, right until the Molotov-Ribbentrop Pact of 1939 put an end to the policy, the Soviet party pursued the major goal of neutralising the Hitler threat. It was the right idea, but the problem was the manner in which it was realised, premised as it was upon a false and distorted image of the main issues in international relations. The fundamental principle adopted by the Soviet leadership in building the anti-Hitler front was a distinction drawn between warlike and peaceable capitalist powers. The danger was to identify the potentially anti-Hitler powers as being progressive *in some more general sense*, rather than in the strictly specific sense of being merely amenable to opposing Hitler. And of course the leading powers in this category, France and Britain, were also the major colonial powers of the day. The argument about the qualitatively more reactionary nature of fascism has a certain truth, but the whole of international relations should not be reduced to this one issue. In effect, the extremely reactionary and oppressive nature of Britain and France in the colonial dimension was entirely downplayed to avoid offending them. This analysis and position would make it extremely difficult for communism to develop a relationship with the progressive forces which were the most fundamental in world politics, and would remain so even after Hitler was dead and gone, i.e. the colonial peoples—most of whom were denied statehood by the colonial system, and thus excluded from the formal world of international relations.

DIMITROV'S REPORT TO THE SEVENTH CONGRESS

The above features and dangers are expressed with particular clarity in what is probably the most important document of the anti-fascist phase of the Comintern—Dimitrov's report to the Seventh World Congress held in 1935. In this report, colonial struggles are dealt with as an afterthought and in an extremely patronising manner. The struggle against European fascism had become not only the key, but also effectively the *sole* task. Dimitrov details a number of social forces which can be enlisted in this struggle, including unity of action with the Socialist International (formerly treated as an enemy of communism), the building of influence over Catholic, anarchist and unorganised workers, as well as workers influenced by fascism, the peasantry, urban petty-bourgeoisie, and intelligentsia of the industrial countries. Only at the end of this long list does he mention the colonial movements, and even here the orientation is one of "transforming the colonies and semi-colonies into one of the most important *reserves of the world proletariat*."[18] This is a total revision of Lenin's picture of the world situation.

While we should not necessarily deny the rationale for a certain "tactical Eurocentrism" aimed to prevent Hitler from launching war, what is wrong is how a qualitative distinction between fascist and democratic forces is presented as the main feature of the world situation. If this strategy implied that colonial peoples should downplay their struggles so as not to annoy the putative anti-Hitler powers then it is even a counter-revolutionary strategy.[19] Earlier Comintern lines had correctly stigmatised the European social-democratic forces for supporting imperialism and colonialism. Now that these forces were potential allies (against fascism) there was a total reversal and they suddenly became okay even though their position in relation to imperialism had not changed. Simply put, this issue was no longer considered important.

Thus began a Eurocentric trend in Soviet thinking on international relations which continued through World War II and beyond. Towards the end of that war, the Soviet Union accepted the Yalta agreement, a proposal made by the British government to stabilise postwar international politics by a mutually accepted delimitation of areas of influence. In order not to rock the boat of this essentially Eurocentric "stability," the Soviet Union even tried to persuade the Communist Party of China not to cross the Yangzi River and liberate the whole of their country, although the Chinese chose to ignore them. Once again, in considering Yalta, we might accept a certain legitimacy in the demand of the USSR—which had made immense sacrifices in the war—to have stable frontiers to the West, thus reducing the likelihood of imperialism launching a renewed attack. The problem is that this assessment overwhelmed everything else, and the whole of world politics was treated as its function. This Eurocentrism, which we might charitably describe in certain contexts as tactical, was in reality strategic. Take, for example, one of Stalin's last works, *Economic Problems of Socialism in the USSR*, published in 1952.[20] The book's scope is a good deal broader than its title might imply and it offers an overview of major issues in the international system. Within this scope, however, the Third World is nowhere to be found. Although, in reality, national movements against colonialism were an outstanding feature of this period, Stalin evidently did not think of them as important.

THE CASE OF THE C.P.G.B.

Having addressed the issue of Soviet foreign policy, we now come to the second of the two trends which adversely affected the Comintern line: the resurgence of social-colonialism within the parties of the imperialist core. As we have said, the overall worldview enshrined in political economy was one which saw the colonial question as relatively unimportant. At best, some superficial lip-service to Lenin might have made it difficult to openly reject the idea of independence for the colonies, but there was definite nervousness at the thought of supporting anti-colonial *movements*. If those movements existed, they should be safely subordinated to, and kept in check by, the metropolitan proletarian "leadership." Perish the thought that these movements should make their own autonomous decisions based on their analysis of their concrete situation and the types of struggle and alliances which this analysis demanded. Effectively, the metropolitan communist parties arrogated to themselves the right to show the oppressed how to respond to their own oppression. A more or less institutionalised tendency existed for the CP of the metropolitan country to exercise a role of tutelage over colonial communists. The slogan of international proletarian solidarity was in this way twisted into its opposite, an excuse for dominance. In a sense, this practice follows logically from the Eurocentric premise which assumes that the metropolitan proletariat is naturally more advanced because it belongs to the industrial phase of history rather than a more "primitive" peasant phase.

Let us consider the case of the Communist Party of Great Britain (CPGB). As late as the close of World War II this party maintained a formally correct position, at least to the extent that it recognised the right of colonial peoples to pursue independence. In practice, however, this position was interpreted in such a way as to forbid any struggle of a type which could *effectively* further such independence. There was no support for the actually existing movements; everything was made to depend on a gesture of the imperialist centre "giving" independence to the colonized periphery; the process of independence was subordinated to, or in fact was treated as a product of, political processes within the core nations. Moreover, this position was premised on completely false assumptions about what these political processes within the imperial centres really were, in other words the shared assumptions of supremacism and colonial "responsibility" which tended to govern relations between the ruling class and the mainstream labour movement.

For example, in one of its documents, the CPGB argues (allegedly taking the standpoint of "British Labour") that, in giving the colonies independence the labour movement "will be following the best traditions of the movement from the earliest times to the present day." The trend opposed to this, which the document criticises, is that of hanging onto empire; this trend, the document alleges, "was in the main the standpoint of a relatively small number of leading personalities such as J.H. Thomas, the last Labour Secretary for the Colonies." On this basis, the document concludes: "there is no question that the former trend [in favour of independence] is the true expression of a Labour outlook and requires only to be developed and put into immediate practical application."[21] It would be very nice if this was true. Indeed, there were moments in the past when it might have been partially true—for instance the stance of the Chartists which was quite progressive on the colonial question—but this analysis wholly neglects the way that the formative period of imperialism had pushed things in the opposite sense, namely a concerted, and to a significant extent successful, drive to recruit mainstream labour into an acceptance of imperial goals. To attribute the chauvinist line to a few rogue individuals is in complete contradiction to Marxism-Leninism, totally subverting the correct point made by Engels to the effect that "the workers gaily share in the feast of England's monopoly of the world market and the Colonies,"[22] let alone the teachings of Lenin.

The CPGB thus not only refused to provide solidarity for the actual struggles of the colonial peoples, it also turned its back on the main form of solidarity which ought to have been built within the metropolis, the only possible basis upon which to recognise and fight the colonial consensus which deeply permeated this "labour movement" in whose interest the CPGB claimed to speak. The viewpoint which sees the centre of the world historical process as being concentrated in the industrial countries obviously cannot recognise the historical importance of the actual struggles *of* the peoples in the colonies themselves.

THE DOCTRINE OF "COMMUNIST RESPONSIBILITY"

Given these flaws, it is not surprising that the formal commitment to colonial independence—which still subsisted in the above-quoted documents—was easily overthrown in favour of something even worse. This shift found its basis in a certain rightist Eurocentric position, which regards the metropolitan movement as "responsible" for the colonies and uses this patronising "responsibility" as a thin disguise for colonialism. In this way, recognition of the evils of imperial rule can be used as an argument to justify *maintaining* that rule in order to provide a chance to undo the evil! A Left Book Club publication in 1945 argues that "[w]here harm has been done, it must be undone ... The problems are so great that for Britain merely to 'give the colonies their freedom' without recognising any further obligations towards them would be cowardice, not generosity."[23]

This line of argument subsequently became the foundation for a shift on the part of the CPGB still further to the right. By 1951, the Party went so far as to argue, in its notorious *British Road to Socialism*, that "[t]he enemies of Communism declare that the Communist Party, by underhand subversive means, is aiming at the destruction of Britain and the British Empire. This is a lie. On the contrary, it is precisely the Tories and Labour leaders who are doing this by their policy of armed repression and colonial exploitation."[24] The CPGB, for its part, calls for "a new, close, voluntary association."[25]

It can be argued that there were issues other than Eurocentrism involved in the degeneration of a party like the CPGB—for example, its espousal of the idea of "peaceful transition" with its hallucinatory notion that the imperialist state would meekly allow itself to be captured by socialist forces. Does our argument imply that these were unimportant? Our answer is that unless we take the issue of Eurocentrism seriously it is difficult to wage a decisive struggle against these other forms of degeneration.

Let us consider more deeply the concept of "peaceful transition" and its expression in the theory of the parliamentary road to socialism. The CPGB has the distinction of being one of the first parties to propagate such a notion—later to be associated with the degeneration of many other parties—to the effect that the capitalist system would voluntarily liquidate itself when faced with the increasing strength of workers' movements operating through mainstream politics.

This trend was in turn part of a wider picture since, in another form of the argument proceeding from similar premises, the economic rise of the Soviet bloc allegedly left international capitalism too weak or demoralised to prevent a stratum of nationalists in the developing world, with an indeterminate class basis, from embarking (with close Soviet assistance) on a path of "non-capitalist development" which would imperceptibly grow into socialism. Thus, it was assumed that the increasing relative economic strength of the Soviet Union *at the level of the world system* would demoralise the capitalists and modify their internal behaviour.

Taking these two forms of peaceful evolution—international and internal—together, it seems the whole world would one day wake up to find itself socialist without either the capitalists or indeed the workers having noticed. Perhaps this seems like a slight parody of the theory, but it is basically true to its essence. The theory of "peaceful transition" presents a very comforting vision but, unfortunately, one that is wholly nonsensical. Moreover, this theory played an absolutely central role in the degeneration of the Soviet-inspired movement, either corrupting radicals or disarming them and leaving them vulnerable to massacres.

What we are arguing is that these errors cannot possibly be understood outside the context of Eurocentrism. For example, the issue of the parliamentary road is not purely such a "domestic" issue as it is sometimes made to appear. There are two aspects in the politics of the imperialist countries: the democratic veneer and the option of militaristic state terrorism which the system holds up its sleeve. Both are closely linked with colonialism: the democratic veneer was made possible by the advantages derived through the exercise of naked terror and superexploitation in other areas of the world, while fascism is the translation into Europe of what has always been practiced in the colonies—another point which Dimitrov's analysis of fascism misses, incidentally. The present-day state machine, and in particular the army, its principal component, has evolved very much in symbiosis with the colonial past, as well as the neo-colonial present. Of course, capitalism has in any case an internally repressive option reserved for situations where it dispenses with the parliamentary veneer. But it is hard to dispute that the concrete form in which this military apparatus has *really evolved* has been in very close connection with external wars and repression in the Global South, whether in a directly colonial form (as with twentieth century Britain and France) or else (in the case of the USA, and in a twenty first century context all the imperialist powers jointly) a neo-colonial one.

The "parliamentary road" theory itself, together with its concomitant theory of the "non-capitalist road," emerged against the background of an analysis of the world system which exaggerated the contradiction between socialist and capitalist countries, underestimating the importance of an economic strength drawn by capitalism precisely through its exploitation of the periphery. The *reserves of strength* which capitalism can draw from this exploitation are sufficient to undermine completely the false notion that the socialist camp would be able to defeat capitalism through economic competition—even if we accept the unrealistic assumption that capitalism would play fairly and accept the result of such competition if it was unfavourable to itself! It is obvious that evolutionary theories of socialism became prevalent in the industrialised countries because of the relative stability of the postwar boom, itself based upon the superexploitation of the rest of the world. Of course, imperialism's reserves of strength are *not invulnerable* — they are indeed vulnerable, but only to the struggles of the mass movement in the periphery, precisely the forces that the Soviet movement was refusing to support because they would rock the boat of its evolutionary theories. All this goes to show that a meaningful critique of the wider phenomenon of the degeneration of the communist line cannot possibly be conducted so long as we are ensnared in Eurocentric premises.

NOTES

1. Lenin, *Selected Works*, Volume 3, 753–4.

2. He was freed the following year, but was arrested again in 1928, suffering further prison terms until his execution in 1940.

3. Lenin, *Collected Works*, Volume 33, 480.

4. Stalin, *Works*, Volume 4, 174–175.

5. Stalin, *Works*, Volume 3, 18.

6. Leontiev, *Political Economy*, 19.

7. Ibid.

8. Lenin, *Imperialism, the Highest stage of Capitalism*, 104.

9. Lenin, *Collected Works*, Volume 38, 363.

10. Communist Party of Great Britain, *Political Economy*, 540–541.

11. Some of the points in this paragraph were suggested by a useful chapter on the general crisis theory in Lotta and Shannon, 245, 253.

12. Dutt was half Indian and half Swedish (from a family which included Swedish premier Olof Palme); he led the CPGB during 1939–41 while Harry Pollitt was temporarily disgraced over his support for Britain's entry into the War.

13. Dutt, 200, emphasis in original.

14. Ibid.

15. See the passage quoted in Forum for Marxist-Leninist Struggle, 2.

16. Dutt, 78.

17. Rodney, 172–173.

18. Dimitrov, 59.

19. George Padmore, one of the most influential Black communists of the inter-war period, broke with the Comintern on this issue. His subsequent positions, as expressed for example in his book *Pan-Africanism or Communism*, are far from being correct, but he was correct at that time in objecting to the subordination of the African struggle to an external Eurocentric strategy.

20. Despite its title this booklet has quite a pragmatic character, and contains an important section on the world situation.

21. Communist Party of Great Britain, *The Colonies*, 55.

22. Marx and Engels, *Selected Correspondence*, 351.

23. Campbell, 8.

24. Quoted in McCreery, 33.

25. Ibid.

China and the Marxist-Leninist Movement

IT was historically inevitable that the world should be jolted out of its Eurocentrism, and the medium for doing this was the revolutionary upsurge in Asia, Africa, and Latin America, particularly in connection with World War II and its aftermath.

In this context, no single event was more important than the Chinese Revolution; its impact on world history in general was paralleled by a possibly even greater impact on the left. Although China did not encapsulate all of the positive trends in the worldwide revolutionary upsurge, it did undoubtedly act as a conduit for the influence of that upsurge within the wider left movement, particularly since the 1960s when the Communist Party of China (CPC) played the leading role in challenging the degeneration of an official Soviet-led movement which had isolated itself from cutting-edge struggles. However absurd, or even quaint, Soviet theories may appear today, in the 1960s they were superficially more plausible; it was therefore to the great credit of the CPC that it led the attack against them. Apart from its struggle against Soviet revisionism, though, the Chinese Revolution represents, by its very existence, a blow against Eurocentrism.

THE IMPORTANCE OF THE CHINESE REVOLUTION

The intrinsically anti-Eurocentric character of the Chinese Revolution can be understood according to the following three aspects. Firstly, the obvious fact that it was a non-European society taking the initiative in making a revolution of historic importance; thus, the revolution proved, exactly as Lenin had predicted, that the centre of creativity could lie outside the "developed" areas. Secondly, Chinese theory and practice had revealed the enormous revolutionary strength of the peasantry, the basic force in the Third World that was reviled and marginalised in Eurocentric thought: the Chinese broke with the non-dialectical infatuation with advanced productive forces producing advanced struggles and demonstrated that the masses' commitment to change in a superexploited oppressed nation was the decisive factor—this represents a blow against mechanistic views of the relationship between base and superstructure, or about a linear succession of historical phases, which are, as we have discussed, closely associated with Eurocentrism. Thirdly, the Chinese Revolution is living proof of the deep historic roots of the progressive movement in the Third World, drawing upon both its pre-colonial roots (the historic dynamism of non-European societies as well as the tradition of struggle by the labouring masses against aspects of oppression within them) and the tradition of national resistance dating back to the earliest foreign incursions; Chinese historiography always stressed the importance of the civilisations and cultures in the non-European areas, as well as the long history of links between them.

In essence, then, the Chinese Revolution represents the necessary process of expanding the boundaries of communism, a theory which had originated in Europe but with a method of *potentially* universal applicability; it changed the entire way people looked at the world. Furthermore, from the beginning of the 1960s, the CPC waged a struggle within the heart of the global communist movement by launching its historic polemic against the errors of the Soviet line which it characterised as "revisionist," a term developed in earlier communist history to describe trends which abandon or revise fundamental and correct aspects of Marxism. Hence, the critique of revisionism was updated and given fresh relevance by the Chinese communists. The whole international movement was shaken up, often in a positive manner. There were nevertheless significant secondary weaknesses of sectarianism, and it will be a complex and necessary task for radical research to assess what was right and wrong in terms of the tactical and strategic form in which that necessary anti-revisionist struggle was waged: for example, significant figures like Che Guevara, who essentially agreed with the substance of the Chinese stance, were critical of the manner in which the polemic was conducted. Since it is beyond our scope to address here the question of strategic and tactical form, we will confine ourselves to analysing only issues of political line. From this angle, it can be argued that probably most of the key propositions advanced by the Chinese were correct, despite significant secondary errors and things left unsaid.

Quite soon after the launching of its polemic against revisionism, the Chinese initiated their Cultural Revolution, the first experiment in a very radical mass movement undertaken *after* the establishment of socialism. The important personal role of Mao Zedong at that time led to the anti-revisionist movement identifying its politics and ideology by the name of Marxism-Leninism-Mao Zedong Thought; the term "Maoism" was often used colloquially, but its meaning had not strictly been explored at that time. This interpenetration of anti-revisionism with the Cultural Revolution added further complications which will again present an important task for future analysis: there were positive and negative aspects; the big weakness was a dogmatism that blocked precisely some of the creative developments which were required (always a risk when one defends purity of line, as the anti-revisionist struggle tended to do).

At the same time there was an overriding positive aspect to this phase of anti-revisionism which, in the long term, will probably outweigh the shortcomings. It is simply the fact that creative developments in theory do not occur in isolation but only on the basis of practice. The strength of Maoism was its assertion that institutional structures, functionaries, intellectuals, etc. must, in the first place, respect the most exploited working masses and thoroughly integrate with them in their life and mode of thinking. If we take this to its logical conclusion, it means seeking out those upon whom the whole structure rests, the most marginalised and exploited. For this reason, it carries with it the potential for the defeat of Eurocentrism. In this sense, we can regard Maoism, like Marxism in general, as the property of humanity as a whole, as something bigger than the limitations of the people who developed it. The positive aspect will survive and, in the future, continue to grow. But in the immediate term its impact was limited by certain weaknesses within the Chinese position.

In order to have a more concrete idea of the main strengths—and limitations—of the CPC's stance following the outbreak of the anti-revisionist struggle, it is interesting to take a look at three sources, which closely relate to the issues addressed in this book. They are: (i) one of the original documents from the Sino-Soviet polemic, the article "Apologists of Neo-Colonialism," first published in 1963; (ii) Mao Zedong's two statements on the African-American struggle, published respectively in August 1963 and April 1968; and (iii) the article *Long Live the Victory of People's War!*, first published in September 1965 under the signature of Lin Biao.[1]

"APOLOGISTS OF NEO-COLONIALISM"

In "Apologists of Neo-Colonialism" the CPC correctly stated that "[t]he storm of the peoples' revolution in Asia, Africa and Latin America requires every political force in the world to take a stand."[2] In general, this article gives an excellent critique of social-chauvinism, the trend which supports imperialist oppression under a "left" guise; the article therefore retains significant topical relevance for the left in the industrialised countries. At the same time, though, it is equally meaningful for the situation in the oppressed nations since it penetratingly critiques the Soviet "non-capitalist" road theory which assumed that change could come without radically struggling against the exploitative order. The article clearly argues that the winning of formal independence by the South, though a significant victory, can easily be subsumed by the global ruling order to form the basis of a new stage of exploitation, "neo-colonialism."

Nevertheless, this position possessed some limitations. Throughout the polemic, the Chinese concentrated on restating basic principles of Leninism from which the Soviet trend had departed. It is perhaps understandable that the Chinese communists saw this as the main front on which the struggle must be waged, and did not want to fight on too many fronts at the same time, but this orientation often detracts from the need to go further, to settle accounts with deeply ingrained weaknesses in the movement which even precede Soviet degeneration, and to break new ground in the application of dialectical and historical materialism.

Thus, the phenomenon really represented by "neo-colonialism" is left rather vague, and in particular is not taken into the realm of political economy. In "Apologists," the content of the term is therefore extremely weak and, insofar as the Chinese do flesh it out, there is an implication of a purely *political* definition in opposition to the CPSU's purely economistic conception of the movement's tasks. Therefore, the dialectical unity of political economy is torn apart into two unrelated aspects, a very dangerous mistake. Moreover, the Chinese were committed to upholding Stalin. Now, as we have argued, there are strengths in this position because Stalin was, initially at least, the most correct member of the Soviet leadership apart from Lenin on the issues in question. For example, in 1925 he made an important intervention warning against the danger of following the "path of nationalism and degeneration" if the Soviet Union were to retreat from supporting the liberation movements and instead engage in power politics. These passages are correctly quoted in "Apologists,"[3] forming a very powerful indictment of the then Soviet leadership. On the other hand, there were other and more problematical aspects of Stalin's heritage. In the Stalin period, there was a second, different definition of nationalist degeneration hovering around: by this we understand, initially, the accusation levelled against the ideas of people like Sultan Galtiev as well as something similar that was to surface in Stalin's last years, when Yugoslavia was kicked out of the socialist camp for such a nationalist deviation in 1948. The Chinese had found themselves, at the time of the Yugoslav expulsion, perhaps overly sensitive to a similar accusation and had taken pains to assure Stalin that *they* were not nationalists like that! The result was, by the time of the polemic against the CPSU in the early '60s, the Chinese had painted themselves into a bit of a corner: they felt vulnerable to accusations of being mere nationalists and uneasy when the argument was conducted on this terrain.

This is particularly important because it meant that the CPC lost the opportunity to attack the Soviets on some of the areas where their degeneration was in fact most intense. In fact the CPSU had, in its attack on nationalism, veered into a space where the racist premises of its thinking peeped through quite brazenly. They even stooped so low as to accuse the Chinese of "playing upon the national and even racial prejudices of the Asian and African peoples" and "creating racial and geographical barriers."[4]

Now, from the kind of standpoint adopted by Lamine Senghor or Sultan Galiev or Li Dazhao, the CPC could have simply thrown the accusation back at the accuser and say, "we didn't 'create' these things: racist exploitation of some areas of the world by others *really* exists and if you can't see this, it's because of your own racism." It is of fundamental importance that colonial peoples should not have to be defensive or apologetic when accused of racism with regard to the oppressor nations. But, for whatever reasons, the Chinese failed to take such a clear stand, and retreated into what sounds like a theological or scholastic defence, which can more or less be paraphrased as: "this isn't really what we really said and, anyway, Marxism doesn't recognise these categories."

In taking such a stance, the CPC in effect rejected the challenge of developing Marxism creatively in this area. The point is surely that if such categories really exist—not of course "race" itself but the category of people superexploited and deprived of human rights according to racially-ascribed determinants—Marxism *should* recognise them! In "Apologists," the CPC therefore sidesteps the issue of racism. They do refer at one point to the way the Russians are resurrecting the "yellow peril" idea, but they fail to counter-attack, as Samir Amin would later do,[5] by arguing that the main historic problem has been a "white peril," which very much includes Russian chauvinism.

MAO ON THE AFRICAN-AMERICAN STRUGGLE

If we now turn to Mao Zedong's statements on the African-American struggle, it can be seen that these confirm the existence of some weaknesses on the issue of racism, combined with Mao's significant strengths. The strong point is that Mao's 1963 statement includes one of the most important sentences on the topic ever written by a communist leader: "[t]he evil system of colonialism and imperialism arose and throve with the enslavement of Negroes and the trade in Negroes, and it will surely come to its end with the complete emancipation of the black people."[6]

In a phrase, Mao thus pinpointed an element which, although formally present in Marx's work, had undoubtedly been completely marginalised in most of communist theory—this was a major achievement. The secondary weakness in Mao's analysis, however, is a strong tendency to see racism, first of all, as merely a kind of policy and, secondly, as one promoted only by the top US leaders. In the same statement, he argued that "it is only the reactionary ruling circles among the whites who oppress the Negro people."[7] This analysis is clearly inadequate. Now, it is interesting that only a couple of months later, Mao was to receive a visit from the Black American activist Robert Williams, who in the course of a rally in Beijing gave a very different, and far stronger, analysis of this crucial question:

> I am aware of the fact that US racism grew out of capitalist exploitation, but today it has become a part of the American way of life. It is a part of the nature of a Yankee. This is not to say that all American whites are racist. Some of them are our brothers and allies, but they are much too few in numbers. No, not all Americans are savages, but we must ask ourselves where are the decent people of the USA while all these atrocities are being committed in the name of their cause of white supremacy and representative democracy?[8]

But Mao's second major statement on the African-American struggle, one published in April 1968 following the assassination of Martin Luther King, showed that he had not fully taken on board these issues, nor progressed decisively from his earlier stance. Here he describes the contradiction "between the black masses ... and US ruling circles" as a class contradiction, claims that "[t]he black masses and the masses of white working peoples in the United States share common interests and have common objectives to struggle for," and predicts that the black struggle "is bound to merge with the American workers' movement."[9] Although, of course, there is not unanimity about what would constitute a correct analysis to counterpose to this perspective, a minimum basis of agreement among progressive trends would probably involve the recognition of facts such as the national dimension of the Black struggle, the qualitatively different oppression suffered by Black people, and the existence of racism amongst ordinary whites. The serious recognition of such issues is undoubtedly a precondition for realising Black-white unity against imperialism. All of these points Mao underestimates.

We will now consider the background to the article *Long Live the Victory of People's War!*, discussed below. In the polemic against the CPSU, the Chinese had moved close to a position where they would have recognised the struggle between the liberation movement of the oppressed and superexploited peoples on the one hand, and imperialism on the other, as the decisive factor in the progress of world history in the present era. Indeed, the Russians tried to goad them into saying this explicitly:

> The chief contradiction of our time is not, we are told, between socialism and imperialism, but between the national liberation movement and imperialism. In the Chinese comrades' opinion, the decisive force in the battle against imperialism is not the socialist world system, and not the international working class struggle but, again we are told, the national liberation movement.[10]

Actually, the Russians were probably correct in saying that this was the logical implication of the Chinese position. In fact, this position is very close to Lenin's statements quoted earlier, and it is an indictment of the CPSU's putrescence that they could think of this argument as something bad! The point is not to deny or downgrade the need for a leading role to be played by the international socialist movement, but simply to recognise that it could retain and develop such a role amongst the world progressive forces—including the liberation movements themselves—only if it recognised that anti-imperialist resistance was the front line of the struggle. But in 1963 the CPC backed away from a clear affirmation that this was indeed what they were saying.

"LONG LIVE THE VICTORY OF PEOPLE'S WAR!"

Two years later, the article *Long Live the Victory of People's War!* at last took a clear stand on the issue. It declared: "[t]he contradiction between the revolutionary peoples of Asia, Africa and Latin America and the imperialists headed by the United States is the principal contradiction in the contemporary world."[11]

The article also found an interesting image to express this contradiction, by expanding onto a world scale a concept which Mao (showing faith in the revolutionary potential of the peasantry) had originally employed to explain the strategy for liberating China: the notion of encircling cities from the countryside. The article expresses this as follows:

> Taking the entire globe, if North America and Western Europe can be called the "cities of the world," then Asia, Africa and Latin America constitute the "rural areas of the world." In a sense, the contemporary world revolution also presents a picture of the encirclement of cities by the rural areas.[12]

These two passages, despite some weaknesses in formulation, are essentially accurate. They are in line with the anti-Eurocentric trend, and are as important to the progressive forces in the industrialised countries as to those in the Third World. Such a strategic vision of the focus of contradictions is essential to the left forces in every region of the globe. In relation to the Global South, it should be noted that (in contrast to the later "Three Worlds Theory") the statement refers to "revolutionary peoples," not to governments. Of course there will be an endemic struggle against the savagery of imperialist exploitation by different strata of society, which is always progressive: nevertheless, this document presents the conscious revolutionary forces with the challenge and responsibility to *lead* this struggle. In relation to the imperialist heartlands, on the other hand, it challenges the revolutionary forces to recognise where the front lines really lie, and to shed any illusions that they can direct the global struggle either ideologically or politically. But this does not of course mean that these forces in oppressor nations should sit back and wait for the oppressed nations to do all the work: on the contrary, the struggle within the heartlands plays an important strategic role, not just in weakening imperialism, but more particularly in terms of the hard work needed to overcome racism/chauvinism and build anti-imperialist solidarity within the working class.

This probably represents the highest point reached by the CPC on such questions; it depicts a world imperialist system built on the backs of the peoples of Asia, Africa, and Latin America who (to paraphrase the *Communist Manifesto*) cannot stir themselves without bringing the whole super-incumbent structure crashing down.

Interestingly, the CPC quickly retreated from this position. The article *Long Live the Victory of People's War!* was signed by Lin Biao, the number two cadre in the Chinese leadership at the height of the Cultural Revolution, and not long after its publication he disappeared, apparently killed in a plane crash while attempting to flee after a failed coup attempt. This affair reflects the abnormal factionalism associated with the Cultural Revolution. In the posthumous critique of Lin Biao which followed, to the best of our knowledge, this article was not significantly implicated and thus probably represented a collective statement of line to which Lin had attached his name. The subsequent retreat cannot therefore be directly attributed to his fall, but the latter did provide the occasion for a general revision of line, and the strong anti-Eurocentric position of *Long Live the Victory of People's War!* was one casualty of this.

The line which eventually replaced it was a curious conception called "Three Worlds Theory." The relationship of this theory to our topic is quite complex. Three Worlds Theory was apparently non-Eurocentric in the sense that it continued to recognise the South (the "Third World") as the main progressive force; it could even be considered a step forward in one sense. *Long Live the Victory of People's War!* had been argued in an idealistic and dogmatic manner. Instead of "seeking truth from facts," the concept of world cities and countryside is derived from another set of ideas, i.e. Mao's concept of Peoples' War. In contrast, Three Worlds Theory was much more tuned in to contemporary reality: it recognised the fact that at that time, in the mid-1970s, there was a movement by *governments* of the Third World for a more just international order, and pinpointed the fact that the USA and the Soviet Union had asserted an unhealthy joint dominance which effectively froze the system under great power control. From a tactical point of view, it was correct to support such a broad anti-hegemonic movement. However, the great weakness of the theory, which completely undermined any progressive aspect, was that it tended to be treated as a guide to *strategy*. In reality, the strategically progressive force was undoubtedly not the Third World national elites but rather the radical left-wing and liberation movements and the broad popular movement whose aspirations were expressed only in a very partial and temporary form at that time by the movement of governments—but they were absent from Three Worlds Theory. From this point onwards, the Chinese line began to lose contact with Leninism.

How could such a switch occur in the space of only a few years? Fundamentally, all the Chinese positions—even at their most correct—were weakened by a lack of creativity in dealing with the basic political economy side of imperialism. At the beginning of the polemic against revisionism there may have been reasons to concentrate on restating Leninist orthodoxy, but as Lenin himself had made abundantly clear, the notion of a frozen and sclerotic "correct" orthodoxy is a contradiction in terms: the only way to defend Marxism was to develop it, primarily by theorising the lessons of the Third World uprising; however, this is just what did not happen. The Cultural Revolution reinforced dogmatism and idealism to the nth degree, making it practically impossible to create the situation Mao envisaged where "a hundred schools of thought contend." The textbooks on political economy which emerged during that period were depressingly dogmatic and harboured practically no original thought.[13] They were basically no better than the "Kautskyite textbooks" Lenin had fulminated against. This fundamental weakness probably explains why the Chinese position was able to degenerate so suddenly into the Three Worlds Theory.

THE MARXIST-LENINIST MOVEMENT

The original Chinese polemic of the 1960s, further intensified by the Cultural Revolution, unleashed a worldwide storm. Although a movement to revitalise socialism was already an objective necessity, it was China's initiative which provided the catalyst. The impact of this impulse of renewal still reverberates, inspiring radical movements in many parts of the world, and is in fact likely to grow and expand its influence in the coming period, for reasons which we will address in the final section.

During its initial phase, the movement—constituted by parties and organisations in many different countries, but possessing nevertheless a strong sense of identity as an international current—typically demarcated itself from the pro-Soviet trend by adopting the name "Marxist-Leninist." In this way, it asserted its commitment to carrying forward the living tradition of revolutionary socialism which the CPSU and its followers had abandoned. The media often labelled this current "pro-Chinese" or "Maoist." The movement itself would at the time mostly not have considered these terms scientific, although many would undoubtedly be proud to be called Maoist, in the sense that they were following Mao's call to "serve the people" and dedicate themselves to the cause of the oppressed, while also learning from his matchless ability to apply dialectics in a concrete way, an ability tested by the historic victory of the Chinese Revolution itself. It would have been premature at that time—as had also been the case with Marxism and Leninism during the period when those theories were still being elaborated—to attempt a scientific summing-up of what Maoism represented. More recently, many revolutionary anti-revisionist movements now do explicitly use the term Maoist.

A critical assessment of the history of Maoism is a fascinating and complex task; it will have to be conducted concretely in the conditions of each country, although there are doubtless some common features. It is beyond our scope to attempt such a critique here but, nevertheless, we will offer a few points relevant to our particular concerns in this book.

The CPC's struggle against revisionism initiated a great international current which has continued right through the half century since the Sino-Soviet polemic of the early 1960s. While this current has been uninterrupted, its development has been tortuous, uneven, and complex. In the case of the Communist Party of the Philippines there has been continuity through most of this period. In India the legacy of the Communist Party of India (M-L), although weakened for a time by repression, has undergone a dramatic resurgence in recent years. The Maoist movement in Nepal has had a significant impact. The Communist Party of Peru (known in the media as the Sendero Luminoso)—which was among the first movements explicitly to attempt a definition of Maoism—had the capitalist state seriously worried for several years. In the imperialist countries, on the other hand, the gains won during the period from the late 1960s through to the early 1980s have been largely dissipated. Since this book is written from the standpoint of radicals working in the imperialist countries, a big issue arises: in order to rebuild the movement, one must begin from a fairly low basis (in terms of theory and traditions). In guiding such a task, and in the interest of future struggles, it is important to understand why the post-1980s degeneration happened; it is reasonable to hypothesise that the question is not unconnected to the issues we have addressed so far.

As we have argued, the pre-Maoist degeneration of official Communism had two sources: one was the errors of the Soviet leadership, which exercised a strong influence worldwide, the other was the pro-imperialist trend in the labour movement of the advanced capitalist countries. The Marxist-Leninist movements in the imperialist countries in that period had a real awareness of these two evils—in fact such an awareness was one of their distinguishing features. Nevertheless, in attempting to deal with these problems concretely, serious weaknesses arose.

Maoists aimed to do two things: learn from the Chinese line, and think for themselves how to apply Marxism-Leninism to their own conditions. This approach was basically correct: on the one hand the CPC's line had immense strengths and (as the initiator of Marxism-Leninism-Maoism) exercised a huge pull; on the other hand, the CPC, to its credit, refused a hegemonic role analogous to that of the Soviets within "their" movement, and constantly drummed into overseas Maoists the need to think independently about their own conditions. But these mainly correct orientations each carried their own dangers. On the one hand, as we have seen, the Chinese line had some weaknesses, which not unexpectedly were carried across into the wider movement. On the other hand, when Marxist-Leninists started thinking for themselves, there was a risk that weaknesses ingrained in the metropolitan labour movements would then raise their head. In some weird way, these two sources of error might even reinforce one another.

In this respect, an interesting case study could be provided by an organisation exceptionally *resistant* to the Chinese "pull": the Communist Party of Britain Marxist-Leninist [CPB-ML].[14] A treasure-house of Eurocentric conceptions can be found in their Second Congress document *The British Working Class and its Party* (1971). The following passage gives something of the flavour:

> The truth is that the more highly industrialised a country is, the more productive is its labour power and the greater is the value produced by its working class. Workers are able through struggle to make some inroads into this value they create in the form of wage

increases—inroads which could not have been made in a non-industrialised economy where the value has not been created. Poverty, therefore, is far greater in the colonial non-industrialised world than it is in a country like Britain. Yet the form that poverty takes varies depending on the level of industrialisation, and there is scarcely a worker in Britain who is more than one wage-packet away from extreme destitution. But if absolute poverty is less in Britain than in the colonial world, the exploitation is no less, for what the workers produce is stolen by the capitalists.[15]

In the above argument, which effectively parrots the mainstream establishment discourse on "underdevelopment," there is no intrinsic link between the fact that one part of the world "happens" to be rich and industrialised, and another poor. The realities of superexploitation, the plunder of natural and human resources, are all shoved aside.

Now, it is true that the Chinese line would not have positively endorsed such rubbish, and in this sense the latter is a direct product of the CPB-ML's effective decision to distance itself as far as possible from the dependent-on-China end of the spectrum—the result being that it simply fell off the radar at the other end, into the worst aspects of labour-movement degeneracy.

But if we ask if the Chinese line was strong enough ideologically to *counteract* such arguments, we could not give an unequivocal "yes." As we have argued, what passed for political economic theory during that period in China was woefully inadequate to analyse the world system underpinning such exploitation. In that sense, they were no better than the CPB-ML. From that angle, China's line offered no reliable guarantee against the reassertion of social-chauvinism in and through the very movement which was meant to fight it.

Not that the M-L movement was soft on the notion of struggle, quite the opposite: under the Cultural Revolution's influence, struggle between lines was even exaggerated and fetishised, sometimes to an unhealthy degree. But interesting issues arise when we try to identify the *point of reference* for such struggle. There was a general feeling of wanting to restore some definition of a "pure," untainted Marxism-Leninism—some sense of returning to a golden age which had prevailed before some kind of "fall." Such a representation makes no sense in terms of history, politics, or dialectics: there could not ever exist some mythical pure orthodoxy which one can simply lie down and bask in; as we have shown, the progressive trend was always (and necessarily) intertwined with its opposite and, however much Marx and Lenin at times came superhumanly close to the correct line, even here this is because of their profound grasp of dialectics. What we should really learn from them is the dialectical method rather than the orthodoxy because then we can apply the method to new conditions.

The dangers of a "golden age" approach, inherently wrong in itself, were further compounded by the simplistic way in which—partly under Chinese influence—it was conceived. Thus, internationally, the "fall" was usually identified with some fateful watershed like the Twentieth Party Congress of the Communist Party of the Soviet Union in 1956 (when Khrushchev denounced Stalin and promulgated the theory of peaceful transition to socialism); in turn, Marxist-Leninists, seeking to adapt this mindset "creatively" to their own conditions, sought some similar hiatus in their own countries. In the case of Britain, this was typically the adoption of the revisionist programme known as *The British Road to Socialism* by the Communist Party in the early 1950s.

Now, the watershed approach is not wholly wrong, and can indeed by very useful if we view it dialectically as a representation of points where quantity passes into quality: *The British Road to Socialism* may arguably indeed have marked such a qualitative step in degeneration. Moreover, the notion of a good communist tradition is also something we should hold onto, and indeed guard as a precious treasure. For example, it should go without saying that we should affirm the progressive character of the struggles waged in the 1920s and '30s and '40s against capitalism, fascism, and (as far as this went) colonialism—this must be emphasised strongly and never forgotten.

But it should be obvious that, in the case of the imperialist countries, the social-chauvinist line was strongly present—and in certain aspects dominant—long before the qualitative point of degeneration. Thus, while the "watershed" idea makes some limited sense, it should not be exaggerated. For example, while it is true that there was a significant change in the 1950s with the abandonment of class struggle, the earlier "left" phases during which the CPGB strongly upheld class struggle (such as the textbooks of the 1930s we have already analysed) were marked by a singular failure to comprehend the colonial basis of the "cake" over which metropolitan workers and bourgeoisie contended.

On this basis, the "anti-revisionist" movement—which in its original form as embodied in the Sino-Soviet polemic could be regarded (with the reservations already outlined) as an authentic and vital two-line struggle—could easily become transformed into a phoney two-line struggle, one which failed to draw lines of demarcation with the real target, imperialist-colonial exploitation. In this case, it would only perpetuate Eurocentrism under a new guise, carrying forward within it that tendency inherited from the pre-1950s movement to vacillate merely between "left" and right forms of social-colonialism. What is needed, therefore, is a strong method, strong criteria, to assess the *long-term* historical context of the left movement in a particular country.

This is unfortunately what the M-L movement mostly lacked. We can illustrate this with an interesting case study, taken precisely from an example where European Maoism *did* seem to be doing what we have just advocated, namely critique a country's communist tradition within its historical framework, and with specific focus on the colonial question. The multi-volume study of the Algerian national revolution and the Communist Party of France by Jacques Jurquet (head of the French ML party) looks as though it should be exactly the right kind of project. But when we read it, the theoretical bankruptcy soon stands woefully exposed.

It should be noted, first of all, that Jurquet's work depended for its impetus upon the lead given by the Chinese in "Apologists of Neo-Colonialism," a work in which the Algerian question is explicitly raised. The French MLs therefore cannot claim too much credit for initiating the critique (in comparison, for example, to British ML debates on Ireland, which were much more a case of people thinking for themselves without waiting for Chinese leadership, and where important successes were scored). Nevertheless, since as we have said, "Apologists" is an excellent document, this at least gave the French what should have been a good starting point. But no sooner does Jurquet venture beyond the bare bones of the Chinese stance, than his analysis becomes erroneous. We will confine ourselves to one instructive example: his treatment of a polemic in the French communist press in the year 1921.[16] Factually, Jurquet's narrative of this exchange is extremely interesting and we can learn a lot from it; but when he tries his hand at analysis, the result lacks clarity.

The debate in question was initiated by the publication of an article (penned by Charles-André Julien[17]) which we can see as very strikingly rightist and racist, referring disdainfully to the "negroes of the Congo, only just removed from cannibalism," arguing in general terms that the nationalism of natives must be approached with some circumspection, but only for the purpose of combatting it more effectively. Nationalist sentiments are viewed as "survivals," as prejudices which have to be done away with; nevertheless, this author argues, such sentiments and prejudices can only effectively be fought on the basis of a careful study and understanding of real conditions in the colonies. The rightist line proposed in this article was subsequently *adopted* by the party as the basis for its position on colonial questions, an important instance of the deeply ingrained chauvinism within the communist tradition. However, this acceptance did not happen unopposed. The article's original publication attracted a strongly-worded polemical rejoinder from a second (anonymous) author, attacking the first article by arguing (with some justification, we might say) that Julien's advocacy of a painstaking concrete study of colonial "realities" is merely an excuse for doing nothing to change them! But what does the second author offer as an alternative to this do-nothing scholasticism? He advocates, as a matter of urgency, "the utilisation of the colonial question in the interests of communist propaganda" and, following the example of the Russians, going into such areas to "exploit the sentiments of national resistance for communist ends"; key to this will be to "awaken among the workers of the colonies the concept of their own class interest, which opposes them to the class of landowners and capitalists and unites them with the metropolitan proletariat."

Jurquet simplistically analyses the above clash as a genuine two-line struggle, but to us it seems to be, rather, a classic case where both sides share the perspective of viewing the colonial peoples as objects of history, adjuncts to the metropolitan struggle. The difference is simply between, on the one hand, considering the "natives" as too backward to make any contribution to the coming battles and, on the other hand, dragooning them into a subordinate role within these battles (one cannot help think, as an analogy, of the way the French bourgeoisie had, shortly before that 1921 debate, press-ganged Africans as virtual beasts of burden during World War I). This so-called line struggle somewhat mirrors that between the exclusionist and assimilationist lines within imperialism. Nowhere in this phoney debate are the liberation struggles of the colonised and semi-(neo)colonised accorded a forward-looking character which, as Lenin recognised, heralds an amazing force on the stage of world history, the voice of whole peoples saying: we are here, we will not be ignored, and we intend to remake the world.

NOTES

1. Lin Biao was installed as number two in the Chinese leadership in 1969, and died in 1971 in a plane crash while attempting to flee to the Soviet Union following an unsuccessful coup attempt. It is possible that the article was in fact the work of a writing group.

2. Communist Party of China, *The Polemic on the General Line of the International Communist Movement*, 187.

3. Ibid., 207–209.

4. Ibid., 212.

5. Amin, "Der Marxismus in Asien und Afrika."

6. Mao, *Statement Calling on the People of the World to Unite*, 6.

7. Ibid., 5.

8. The speech is printed among the "supplementary material" in ibid., 84.

9. Mao, *Statement by Comrade Mao Tse Tung*, 3–4.

10. Communist Party of China, *The Polemic on the General Line of the International Communist Movement*, 201.

11. Lin, 53.

12. Ibid.

13. For example, *L'Impérialisme Aujourd'hui* (1976), translated from a Chinese text published around 1974–5, is basically disappointing and contains hardly anything original. A similar criticism would apply to other textbooks from the same source, e.g. *Etudions l'Economie politique*.

14. The Communist Party of Britain (Marxist Leninist), headed by Reginald Birch, was once the best known organisation in the Maoist movement in Britain, and caused significant

confusion around 1970 at a time when relatively large numbers of people were interested in Marxism-Leninism. Its line was thoroughly riddled with social-chauvinism, but this fact was not deeply grasped, even by many of its critics.

15. Communist Party of Britain (Marxist-Leninist), 6.

16. Jurquet, 100–109.

17. Charles-André Julien was for a time a significant figure in the Comintern, and attended its 1921 Congress; subsequently, he abandoned communism and was a member of the Parti socialiste.

Towards a Dialectical Appreciation of the Anti-Eurocentric Current of Theory

ON the positive side, the post-World War II period did witness a real thrust in the direction of the long-awaited creative development of theory. In a few cases, the people who did this also held institutional leading roles: Che Guevara and Amilcar Cabral are outstanding examples, whose legacy is still undiminished. Unfortunately, however, important creative thinking has too often been isolated from the organised movement: the result has been a gap between theory and practice.

In the case of pro-Soviet groups, it is hardly surprising that creativity was frowned and stamped upon: there was an ingrained institutional hatred of anti-Eurocentric ideas, which somehow they viewed as threatening. What is more strange, and this is perhaps the thing which (among all the histories we are recounting in this book) an observer from Mars might find most baffling, is that creative thought was also weakly integrated with the pro-Chinese trend, which one might think would be its natural home. There is no denying that the impetus provided by the CPC's anti-revisionist polemic played a big role in creating conditions for a breakthrough: it tore away the icy grip of Soviet dogmatism, and it is no accident that a huge critical movement of ideas developed in its wake. But there is also a sense in which Maoism on the one hand, and the creative development of political economy on the other, ran somehow parallel to one another, contemporaneous but not converging or cross-fertilising as they should. Such failure could have been avoided if the subjective factors had been stronger. But even if it is not inevitable, such a disconnection is certainly *explicable* given the background issues which we have addressed throughout this book.

The focal issue of the theoretical movement was the reality of the exploitation and struggles in the South. Many of the leading thinkers were people from oppressed nationalities and were sensitive to grassroots issues, even if organisational leaderships were wary of them. Even where the theoretical developments occurred in the North, as in the important contribution of the independent Marxist journal *Monthly Review*, they were often inspired by a reflection on the reality of exploitation and struggle in the periphery.

A certain focus to the development of a non-Eurocentric theory was provided by the trend known as dependency theory, which came into existence from the late 1960s onwards. Such a great theoretical movement was obviously not homogeneous: the dependency trend developed through vigorous internal debates, precisely the kind of debates which ought to have been welcomed much earlier within the official movement, but which had in practice been excluded since the early 1920s. It is therefore natural that among the key contributors were people who would disagree with important aspects of our own interpretation, for example Andre Gunder Frank and his stance on the national question. Nevertheless, I believe we are justified in regarding dependency theory as a realisation of the anti-Eurocentric trend expressed in this study; this is particularly so because the person who can reasonably be considered its central figure, the Egyptian theorist Samir Amin, sums up many of the progressive currents in a comprehensive way.

To claim that dependency theory was somehow a "realisation"

of the anti-Eurocentric trend in political economy does not imply *finality;* the theoretical movement is an ongoing one because the real situation in the twenty first century is significantly different from what it was in the 1970s, making it necessary to creatively adapt the tools of that tradition and build a new stage of theory appropriate to these conditions. But this is itself a tribute to dependency theory's success (despite some important limitations, for example on the issues of gender and the environment), in laying a sound basis for the further development of theory.

The dependency perspective made it possible to understand what is in some sense the key issue in anti-Eurocentrism, namely the interdependence between imperialist centre and colonial periphery in the mechanisms of exploitation and class politics. Marx had revealed two important tendencies within the core: first, the remuneration of labour is not fixed by absolute laws, so workers could and should struggle to obtain a better deal within the boundaries of the current system (while maintaining a strategic objective of an *alternative* system); second, because the essence of capitalism is accumulation (meaning among other things the concentration of wealth in few hands), the progress of the system inevitably brings with it "pauperisation," the expansion of poverty. In the twentieth-century context, capitalism faced an important dilemma with respect to these two tendencies: it would have an interest in establishing a dialogue with the co-optable facet of the labour movement, thereby consolidating itself socially, while also creating an indispensable market for the new mass-produced goods by pushing consumerism, but this would restrict the rate of profit too much. The solution was to internationalise the contradiction, permitting the mass market in the core to grow while the poverty-creating aspect, which limited consumerism, was banished to the periphery. It was thus in the periphery that, as Samir Amin expressed it, "the absolute pauperisation of the producers exploited by capital manifests itself in all its brutality. But it is precisely here that the pro-imperialist tendency within Marxism stops short, because it is from here on that Marxism becomes subversive."[1] This is an extremely important and historic statement. The understanding of these realities is subversive because it brings us closer to the actual situation, stripping away the ideological veils and all the denial: only by acknowledging the reality of these relations can they be challenged. The problem of poverty in the South—bafflingly intractable for the mainstream "development" discourse—stands revealed as intrinsic to accumulation itself. Such an advance in understanding could not possibly have occurred through abstract academic reflection, but only because the dependency authors were tuned in to the real situation in the periphery, the suffering of the masses, the resistance to which this gives rise, and the fundamental exploitative mechanisms which this resistance probes and exposes. Such a recognition is very explicit in Amin's work.

Dependency theory was in turn part of a broader current of Third Worldism. The aspect which touches most closely on the issues addressed by us was the tradition of radical Black thought, which continued to develop on the basis of its already deep roots, and flourished in a mutually-beneficial relationship with dependency theory: the links between the two currents are explicit in the work of Walter Rodney. The Marxist core within this current remained as a crucial element, drawing on the traditions of earlier radicals, both representatives within the official movement, like W.E.B. Du Bois, and ones who had been pushed into minority tendencies because of the official movement's hostility, like C.L.R. James.

At the same time, many important contributions to the radical Black tradition came from thinkers who were not Marxists. As people directly experiencing oppression, they could often see things much more clearly than Marxists who were relatively insulated. This is to some extent bound to be the case, but it was obviously accentuated in circumstances where official communist leaderships did not comprehend Black liberation. These contributions of Black thinkers were linked to major mass movements, in particular the Black movements in the USA, and the Africanist movements in Azania (South Africa).

A key issue was a much deeper understanding of the sense in which capitalism/colonialism was not progressive, in which it set back the cause of humanity. This could never have been perceived so clearly from within the core. In fact it is only from the standpoint of the colonised that the damage wrought by capitalism in general can fully be understood. It is not just the exploited areas themselves who suffered, but the whole future scope of human development: the main reason is homogenisation, the suppression of variety—which reached a further stage with globalisation. On this subject, Mahmadou Dia has pointed out that the colonial division of labour represents "a deterioration of world economy, in its capacity as manifestation of the universal, and ... the consolidation of hegemonies,"[2] and Susantha Goonatilake, in his important critique of the process of "hegemonic cultural blanketing," points out that "[c]ultural diversity is an array of responses to changes in the socio-economic environment and its elimination implies that the learned responses at the world's command will be fewer."[3]

Of course, we still have to use our heads in analysing the trends of Third Worldism and Black consciousness, and should no more accept them uncritically than we have trends within the official movement. We could take the case of Cheikh Anta Diop who, in an important sense, is more Marxist than most mainstream Marxists: without claiming to follow historical materialism, his affirmation of the historicity of African civilisations has made one of the biggest contributions imaginable *to* historical materialism. At the same time, there are limitations in Diop's conceptual framework—presumably limitations of class stance, which actually undermine his ability to draw the conclusions which are crying out to be drawn from his own findings. Let us consider how this manifests itself in relation to a key issue: the dynamism of pre-colonial societies. It is precisely their dynamism, their ability to develop and change, which colonisers feared, because it undermined the Eurocentric myth of stagnation. But Diop, in *L'Afrique noire précoloniale*, practically accepts the concept of stagnancy, or at least "immobility," of African society, regarding it as a virtue because it supposedly preserved the continent from the disruptive influence of class.[4]

We may explain Diop's strange acceptance of what seems to be a colonial stereotype by suggesting that the class stance of the elites in relation to *contemporary* society provides a distorting lens when they regard *traditional* society. In the contemporary situation they don't wish to acknowledge class struggle because this has uncomfortable implications for their own status; they therefore deny the evidence of social conflict in early society. But because it was precisely social contradiction which constituted the basis of pre-colonial dynamism, they are therefore denying dynamism itself! This is an interesting logical progression, which shows clearly why the Marxist perspective is needed. What elites fear is the radical current in the national movement, a current which constitutes the carrying-forward, in a very new form, of the sceptical, anti-authoritarian trend always present within traditional society. Of course, the strategic target of the mass movement is now foreign domination and exploitation, but its immediate orientation is usually to expose and critique the elites' inadequacies (at best) in leading the national movement *against* that exploitation, or at worst (very frequently) their sell-out policies and collusion with exploitation. Class politics does not necessarily mean sectarianism or some kind of Troskyite absolutising of working-class struggle against anything and everything; the elites still have their place within the cause, as it was very well defined by Amin (drawing upon Mao's theory of New Democracy): that of forming a progressive bloc of classes in opposition to the hegemonic bloc which sustains the imperialist system. But they would have to accept leadership from the grassroots, and this their ideologues find difficult to contemplate. Ayi Kwei Armah spills the beans and reveals the Third World bourgeoisie's fear of their own working class when he writes: "[t]he miner's work in Africa is to assist the invading Western pirate in the robbery of his motherland. This makes the former at best a zombie; at worst a culpable accomplice, the hard-working and perennially short-changed sidekick of the

Western mugger."[5]

Conveniently, Armah's argument alleges that, in the African context, the worker is reactionary and the bourgeoisie the main force for progress! The attack on Eurocentrism is thus twisted into an argument that classes—and more broadly, the notion of internal contradictions within society—are an artifical import, imposed upon the South and having no place there. According to this line of argument, the goal of anti-Eurocentrism would be to re-establish the healthy values of a society free from internal contradiction, a deceptive discourse which has always served as a tool to bolster oppression. As self-anointed "natural" leaders of the national movement, the elites would presumably be the interpreters of this allegedly healthy, struggle-free tradition. Distorted and truncated in this way, cultural nationalism is something imperialism would happily accommodate.

Such an aversion to working-class struggle typifies the class position underlying the whole trend. We must of course continue to respect the significant difference between, on the one hand, a great thinker like Diop and, on the other, professional anti-communists like Carlos Moore. Nevertheless, it remains true that non-Marxism always threatens to veer at some point into *anti*-Marxism. If you argue that the very *idea* of social contradiction, of struggle against actual or potential exploitation, is itself a pernicious European import, then it is safest to keep these dangerous heresies away from the African masses. This inevitably carries a reactionary streak, not too distant from the anti-communism which has always been propagated by world capitalism, whether in the 1840s, after 1917, during the Cold War or today. In opposition to the argument that communism (political economy, class politics) is of no use to Africans, we argue: those who suffer from the most intense aspects of exploitation will be the best and most creative Marxists; the vocation of communism is to be taken up by the Third World and developed into a truly universal system of thought.

In the absence of a historical materialist theory of development, how can one explain development at all? One is inevitably thrown back upon either the unconvincing myth of a completely static world with no contradictions, or upon some disguised variant of what are in fact the Eurocentric distortions which the Africanist trend is supposed to combat. An example of this is Social Darwinism. Taharka, in his book *Black Manhood*, makes a useful contribution by marshalling the evidence to demonstrate the essentially African character of ancient Egyptian civilisation but fails to express any alternative to the Eurocentric concept of the dynamic of social development; this can be seen in his parroting of the most extreme arguments about female inferiority which hardly differ from the pseudo-scientific evolutionist ideas about the inequality of so-called races.[6] Feminism is here also viewed as a Eurocentric importation!

We have argued that a historical materialist perspective is essential, but still need to be more specific about what this means. The non-Marxist (anti-Marxist) critique of the notion of modes of production is rarely honest, and tends to fabricate a distorted and stultified image of the thing it wants to attack. Nevertheless, as our argument has shown, this is complicated by the fact that there are indeed distortions, if not in the basic philosophy of dialectical and historical materialism itself, then at least in the expression imposed on it by the limitations of the geographical-historical background against which it concretely developed. The difficulty of disentangling complex situations like this is precisely why it is necessary to push the boundaries of our understanding of Eurocentrism further.

In attempting to address this problematic, it is very useful to take as our central issue the role of slavery. Why does something so apparently "primitive" occur within a "modern" mode of production like capitalism: what on earth is it doing there — surely it ought to have been superseded by the onward march of modes of production? Faced with this awkward question, should we retreat into denial or, on the contrary, seize the opportunity to make ourselves ask uncomfortable but ultimately productive questions about the fundamental realities of both capitalism and the dialectics of history in general?

In a well-known passage in the first volume of *Capital*, Marx refers to the process of primitive accumulation through colonialism and the slave trade as the "rosy dawn" of the capitalist era.[7] Moore, in a deliberate distortion, pretends to take this passage at face value, as though Marx were being serious, but of course it is really a bitterly ironic expression similar to the term "civilisation-mongers," used by Marx elsewhere to stigmatise colonialists. In another important passage, Marx says that "[d]irect Slavery is just as much the pivot of bourgeois industry as machinery, credit, etc."[8] Here again, Moore twists the sense, implying that Marx meant this is a good thing by pushing forward a unilinear scenario of progress within which capitalism plays an indispensible progressive role. However, that is not at all what Marx meant. In fact, the statement in question is perfectly accurate, and indeed constitutes one of Marx's significant insights. The point, subsequently confirmed by the research of Eric Williams, Walter Rodney, etc., is that slavery was indeed the pivot of bourgeois industry.

There is, moreover, an interesting subtext revealed by the specific context in which Marx first articulated the "bourgeois industry" argument: as part of his polemic against Proudhon. The point for Marx was to draw lines of demarcation with reformism. In opposition to Proudhon's cosy supposition that justice could be won by eliminating the *abuses* of the present system, Marx argued that the system *as a system* must be smashed. The atrocities and abuses, including apparently anachronistic forms dredged from the entrails of exploitation's historical recesses (of which slavery is here taken as an example) are an integral and intrinsic part of capitalism *qua* system. This remains a powerfully correct argument. The global system still thrives on superexploited labour, of which indentured forms are close to slavery and all sorts of atrocities are used to keep the masses in order—whether it is death squads, dungeons or other oppressive measures. The significance of these primitively savage repressive methods has only increased with globalisation and outsourcing.

In this sense, Marx is absolutely right. Nevertheless, there are still criticisms we can make of his stance which can be summarised under two general categories. Firstly, although we *can* find these brilliant statements in his work, he did not emphasise such ideas enough. Recognition of the fundamental role of colonialism and the slave trade is sufficiently peripheral in his work that the later Eurocentric trends were able to conveniently ignore it; this is precisely why Du Bois, C.L.R. James, etc. had to fight so hard to re-establish this truth. However, there is also, secondly, the somewhat different problem which surfaces in relation to his critique of Proudhon's reformism. While *at a strategic level* Marx is right (that you have to get rid of the system itself in order to eliminate its abuses), at the level of day-to-day struggle the issue of reformism has to be assessed differently. Assuming you have a sound strategic vision (i.e. you recognise that ultimately it is the system itself which should be trashed), struggles to limit particular abuses are very much progressive and necessary, and in fact contribute to the strategic goal by building the forces and movements of struggle. Even small reformist victories can empower the masses, and the fact that the bourgeoisie will seek to usurp the fruits of such struggles is not an excuse for not waging them. Marx understood this perfectly well when dealing with other causes such as the movement against absolutism or mercantilism, and in a similar spirit he did back the North in the American Civil War. But this does not go deep enough, because slavery is an issue of human rights, not just of tactics. Part of humanity was being excluded from humanity, an issue which Marx might have addressed in relation to his theory of alienation. On this basis, we would then see that the correct way to relate to abolitionism was to build a movement centred not on the bourgeois liberals (though the latter might be an adjunct to it) but on the resistance of the slaves themselves, whereby alienation is overcome and their humanity re-asserted. But, as we have seen, this is just what Marx failed to do. It is against this background that we can appreciate the full significance of the contribution of the Black Marxist trend.

Cedric Robinson provides a superb summing up of Du Bois's thought on this question:

> No theory of history which conceptualised capitalism as a progressive historical force, qualitatively increasing the mastery of human beings over the material bases of their existence, was adequate to the task of making the experiences of the modern world comprehensible. For Du Bois, America in the first half of the nineteenth century, a society in which manufacturing and industrial capitalism had been married to slave production, had been a microcosm of the world system. The advanced sectors of the world economy could expand just so long as they could dominate and rationalise by brute force the exploitation of essentially non-industrial and agrarian labour. The expansion of American slavery in the 19th century was not an anachronism but a forewarning.[9]

The implications of this brilliant concept need to be reflected upon carefully. Robinson himself, as a non-Marxist conducting a historiography of Marxism, has evidently not done so since he writes: "Hegel's dialectic of *Aufhebung*, Marx's dialectic of class struggle and the contradictions between the mode and relations of production, Darwin's evolution of the species and Spencer's survival of the fittest are all forged from the same metaphysical conventions."[10] The fundamental error here is that, for reasons of class stance, Robinson assumes the notion of mode of production to be *inherently* Eurocentric. This is not at all true to the spirit of Black Marxism. Far from throwing the baby of historical materialism out with the bathwater of Eurocentrism, the contribution of Black Marxism was to restore the true potential to the theory by stripping away its Eurocentric distortions.

While there were limitations in Marx and Engels' understanding of non-European modes of production, and of the interaction between different modes internationally during the period of the growth of capitalism, the basic Marxist standpoint was mainly consistent with dialectics. The same cannot be said for subsequent developments of official communist theory; here, we find a strong tendency towards a dogmatic and mechanical model where in all circumstances there must be a rigid succession of the following five distinct modes, viz. primitive communism, slave society, feudalism, capitalism, and communism (with the proviso that societies at more "primitive" stages could, under the aegis of the USSR, skip a stage or two on the road to socialism).

On the one hand, the above understanding of history is pure Eurocentrism, and constitutes a blatant revision of Marx who was fully aware that whatever he could say about *specific* modes of production was limited by the European context of his theories.[11] Most astonishingly, the notion of an Asiatic mode of production (quite an important element in Marx's thinking which, although incorrect in some respects, reflects at least a consciousness of the need to think in specific ways about non-European societies) was banished from the rigid orthodoxy.[12] On the other hand, this dogma of succession is impossibly unilinear, reductionist, and mechanistic: although it is correct to recognise *some* succession of modes of production, Marx would never have dreamed of anything so dogmatic. In fact, these two critiques of the mode of production dogma are intrinsically related, insofar as — something we have already noted at many points of this study — there is a *necessary* connection between Eurocentrism and the distortion of dialectics. Eurocentrism inherently implies mechanical and non-dialectical attitudes to history, development, world politics, etc., simply because it depicts the core (the West/North) as the sole source of dynamism, and the capitalist and imperialistic dominance of that core as justified, or at least inevitable.

The Africanists, in liberating themselves, can contribute immensely to liberating the whole of humanity from these dual distortions of dialectics. This works in the following way: the starting point is the history of slavery, but this in turn says something broader about the whole notion of progress. Whatever progression has occurred through the succession of modes of production not only negates, but at the same time subsumes, earlier forms of exploitation. While there may indeed be progressive *aspects* in this developmental process, such as the assertion of human rights through the destruction of feudalism, there was always a tendency for these to be accompanied by a resurgence of more savage, primitive forms of exploitation. Imperialism, by destroying the functioning traditional societies (albeit in some cases hierarchical ones) while denying the possibility of replacing them with any viable alternative, opened the way to horrendous oppression and abuses, of a type which still underpins world capitalism.

In this sense, what Du Bois is saying is fully in accord with dialectics, and in fact constitutes an excellent example of the Hegelian concept of the negation of the negation. This has implications beyond even the issue of the slave trade, which was our starting point. For example, European feudalism negated classical autocracy in favour of a diffuse, hierarchical power structure; when capitalism in turn negated this, the somewhat progressive aspect of bourgeois democracy was accompanied by a resurgence of the suppressed absolutist power of the state, which carried with it the potential for far greater oppression and militarism. Another example of the non-unilinear, dialectical view is Samir Amin's demonstration of the fact that European world dominance was the result, not of the *advanced* character of its civilisation, but precisely of the backwardness and incompleteness of the social system prevalent there at the dawn of the capitalist era—namely, feudalism, a marginal form of a wider family of "tributary" modes of production, whose very incompleteness meant that it provided less resistance to the growth of capitalist relations of production than in other societies.

The Marxist Africanist perspective provides the starting point not only for a non-unilinear view of development, but also for appreciating the inherent dualism within capitalism, whereby "modern" forms of exploitation co-exist with "primitive" ones. In more recent periods the same dualism recurs, for example in the treatment of "illegal" migrants. Here, too, the achievement of non-Eurocentric theory is not to destroy the concept of class struggle, but to appreciate it in a fuller sense. And this takes us back to the class-nation issue.

It would be sterile to counterpose, on the one hand, an economistic vision of class struggle (supposedly conducted in the economic realm) and, on the other, a national movement, as though they come from different realms. Both have a basis in economic exploitation, but in both cases strong ideological and cultural factors play an autonomous role. While unifying the two concepts within a single paradigm, we simultaneously re-emphasise the need for a firm understanding of the fundamental dualism within capitalism. In the last analysis, the national question is only one manifestation of such a dualism, whereby capital exploits different forms of labour in different ways, according to determinations which it imposes on certain groups. Exploitation in the periphery is part of the same phenomenon as class and, at the same time, qualitatively more intense because determinants—"race," gender, possession of a passport, etc.—are superimposed. Because people subject to these determinations are not only *paid* less, but also work and live under repressive and unsafe conditions and are subject to physical aggression and threat, we can say that the differential is not merely economic, but is a qualitative issue of valuing them less as human beings, of denying their human rights and even their humanity itself. This is a profoundly embedded feature of capitalism: it can never "modernise" itself away from these differentials, nor would it have an interest in trying. The fact that these differentials are accepted unquestioningly shows that they are deeply embedded within the total life of societies, within the whole experience garnered by oppressor societies through colonialism. This demonstrates the autonomous role of the ideological sphere within a truly dialectical reading of modes of production.

Capitalism exploits in ways that are not purely capitalist—this was a crucial realisation which builds from the Black Marxist position on colonialism and slavery. One way of understanding this realisation is provided by dependency theory's application of the concept "social formation" which demonstrates that elements of different modes of production could exist side-by-side under the auspices of a dominant mode. This theory builds on the mode of production idea but provides a bridge to its real world application, both in terms of theoretical breakthroughs and in guiding practice—showing in concrete situations how capitalism maintains dualism, "special" forms of exploitation salvaged from the worst aspects of earlier modes.

As the dominant mode on a world scale, capitalism writes the rules even—and especially—for those not admitted to the sphere of its pure relations or even accorded *recognition* by those rules. In a way, the more general phenomenon of which Eurocentrism is an expression signifies the existence of a centre which sets the rules of an order for its own benefit and imposes it upon those on the margins. It does so not just globally but within the imperialist states themselves, for example in the very important non-remunerated or under-remunerated labour performed by women and racially-determined oppressed groups.

This relationship is the general basis of the national question, but the national contradiction also expresses itself under an immediate, and in fact somewhat superficial, form: *the frustrations of the local bourgeoisie* who, although partly co-opted by the global order and receiving certain crumbs from it—even in some cases significant enough agglomerations of crumbs to add up to a sizeable slice of cake!—nevertheless chafe under their exclusion from effective decision-making. A major weakness in the mainstream communist approach has been to mistake this form as the *essence* of the national question. This could be seen, for example, in the '20s and '30s when all the intense debates on the national question tended to reduce it to this particular aspect—a bourgeois campaign which (depending on the international circumstances, or whether a leftist or rightist line prevailed at a particular time) communism was supposed either to support or not support.

The reality was always different. Neither the progressive nor the reactionary facet of the national movement can be understood on the basis of a Eurocentric political economy. The progressive aspect is that the national independence movements (in their deepest sense a struggle by the masses albeit often under elite leadership) did indeed play a major historical role, but the Comintern stance did not even provide a very good basis for appreciating what this really was. It was always more than a mere economic movement, possessing a profound human rights aspect. The imperialist countries have always consistently opposed even those changes which the system subsequently revealed itself well able to accommodate: for example, on the principle "if it ain't broke don't fix it," they would have quite happily continued with direct colonial rule. Viewed in this way, the independence movement, whatever its leadership, raised fundamental questions of democracy, human dignity, the right to a decent and secure existence, and the overthrow of the racist, oppressive power-structures of international relations.

On the other hand, the bourgeois form of nationalism is something which, however much imperialism may find it a nuisance at times, it has mainly learned to handle. The first attempt was under colonialism, which developed many ways of co-opting local rulers, but it was rather primitive and inefficient: it was so *obviously* racist that large cross-class coalitions developed against it, in the shape of the national independence movements. The second attempt was neo-colonialism, the system established through the recognition of colonial independence after World War II; this created a convincing simulacrum of national capitalist development which, however, ran out of steam by the 1970s at which point another cross-class alliance emerged in the shape of the "Third World movement." But the system simply defused it by acceding to the key bourgeois demand, i.e. access to Northern markets for manufactured exports, and turning this into a big source of profit for itself. This created the basis for the third and current stage: so-called globalisation. In this form, instead of the (phoney) promise that elites will be admitted to the charmed circle via the development of their *nations*, these elites are seemingly integrated *directly* into a kind of transnational global ruling class (though obviously in a subordinate role) and lose their roots in local society and culture. However, while imperialism's co-optation tactics have certainly weakened the national movement in this superficial sense, there has always been another, profounder aspect which remains radical and difficult to co-opt.

The real essence of the national movement has always been something which goes far beyond the stultified definition of human rights merely as a de-racialised access to the spoils of plundering nature and humanity. It is rather a struggle to re-establish the intimate relationship of the working people with their own land, the connection between land, culture, and language, the human need for a dis-alienated relationship to the products of one's own toil, the importance of being strong in oneself and drawing upon one's own human resources. In one sense, this is simply an aspect of a general movement by humanity to rebuild such relationships, to reverse the alienation wrought by capitalism. For example, in every part of the world, the industrial system has distorted life by severing it from the land. However, it is obvious that in the case of the peoples oppressed by imperialism and colonialism, the destruction has been qualitatively more intense. This is why an important aspect of this working people's movement is necessarily national in form and finds a crucial point of reference in a specific land, language, and culture.

If in some respects this cause seems to look to the past, this is only because the act of colonisation always robbed people of their history. It is necessary to reconnect with the pre-colonial creativity, the tradition of earlier liberation struggles, as well as coming to terms with the pain of genocides, all of which have been written out of official history. But the movement is not fundamentally backward-looking; it remains open to the future in the sense that it comprises, as a fundamental part of its makeup, a critical dialogue with tradition: traditional cultures themselves had strong aspects of alienation, for example with respect to gender. Similarly, the movement is not fundamentally *inward*-looking. It necessarily implies an aspiration to self-reliance, but this in no way translates into introspection or autarky, still less into narrow nationalism or xenophobia. The whole point is that the national movement is a contingent of a wider, international struggle, and precisely because it targets the most intense form of capitalist alienation, it is in the front line of that struggle. It is thus simultaneously rooted in and open to the world. The new phase of alienation associated with "globalisation" has in some respects taken this creative relationship between groundedness and openness to a higher level, as one can see in the Mexican Zapatistas. Migration and the constitution of diasporas, though a product of oppression, are also a source of strength, and this again acts in the sense of openness.

The national movement necessarily faces new tasks. These can be faced by the liberation movement in the sense in which we have defined it, as something forward-looking and outward looking. Globalisation has created an unprecedented alienation, and placed on the agenda a re-capturing of culture. The indigenous production of knowledge has always been the root of a *sustainable* definition of science and technology. Science, under the dominance of capital, has completely lost any sense of social responsibility. The land is still the essence: capitalism has robbed humanity as a whole of its contact with the land, but it is contemporary movements like the movement of the landless which act as a force for *resolving* that alienation. The aspect of openness acts as a melting pot for many progressive ideas which may be needed to critique the narrowness or oppressive aspects of tradition. The national movement is therefore not, and has never been, intrinsically bourgeois. On the contrary, it is likely to be the dependent ruling classes who, in collaboration with imperialism, side-track it into divisive or fundamentalist forms. Within the resistance movement, including its national form, there therefore exists contradiction. It is the masses, the most marginalised, who push it in a radical direction, towards self-reliance.

On the basis of these fundamental relationships, the national movement may, from time to time, take the form of a struggle led by either traditional or modern rulers, either to resist imperialist invasions or to claim the reality of a national economic development which the system hypocritically offers, but on racial grounds actually refuses. The communist movement was correct to say that such struggles should—in the right circumstances—be supported, but (apart from Lenin) it never had a very strong basis for understanding the distinction between the ruling-class politics which sometimes gives it expression, and the deeper popular current of which they are merely an imperfect and temporary expression.

In fact, the assumption that the national movement is inherently capitalist never made much sense. The Eurocentric idea of a necessary progression through the same stages as the "classic" industrial revolutions forgets the fact that the latter were based not just upon accumulation of a surplus from the domestic labouring population, but upon colonial exploitation and the slave trade, while the process of capitalist nation-building involved the violent homogenisation of the now-existing states through the suppression of minorities as well as a process of the most devastating wars with rival powers, stretching over many centuries. Logically, this paradigm could never be the basis of a *generalised* development of the South. Nor could global capitalism *permit* such a development, since the existence of some periphery is an indispensible condition not only for the *origins* of capitalist development, but also for its *continuation*.

In an important sense, the analysis of the national question is linked with the analysis of democracy. There has been a significant tendency within the movement to identify the democratic movement itself as "bourgeois," as an expression of the limited progressive character of the bourgeoisie: firstly, in opposition to feudalism; secondly, in opposition to imperialism. This assumption is highly dubious. Once again, it is a question of distinguishing between form and substance. There is a contingent form which is bourgeois, but the implications of democracy reach far beyond its contingent bourgeois form. If one surveys the *reality* of the world system, it is the mass movement of the marginalised which is posing the important questions about the future direction of history. The top-down nature of state power in the periphery had seemed adequate for the earlier national struggles, based on the goodwill and trust which national independence leaders had won from the masses. But it was ultimately inadequate because the victories could not be consolidated. In fact, the last few years have seen a counter-attack by imperialism aimed at recuperating those areas where the national bourgeoisie had temporarily increased the strength of the Third World relative to imperialism through such factors as nationalisation of resources and raising petroleum prices. Neo-liberalism's role was to shut down any scope for debate within the existing political apparatus, imposing a sham pluralism premised on unquestioning acceptance of a single dogma. Thus, the implications of democratisation are very far-reaching: the alternative can only be to build from below.

NOTES

1. Amin, *La Loi de la valeur et le matérialisme historique*, 36. The published English translation distorts the sense of this passage.

2. Dia, 28.

3. Goonatilake, v.

4. Diop, 5, 7.

5. Armah, 64.

6. Thus, according to Taharka, the male qualities, developed over a long period of evolution include "aggressiveness, strength, speed, endurance, courage, agility, a sharpening of the intellect, resourcefulness and good co-ordination," whereas females for their part are simply endowed with "a greater amount of maternal instinct." (Taharka, 5–6)

7. "The discovery of gold and silver in America, the extirpation, enslavement and entombment in mines of the aboriginal population, the beginning of the conquest and looting of the East Indies, the turning of Africa into a warren for the commercial hunting of black skins signalised the rosy dawn of the era of capitalist production. These idyllic proceedings are the chief momenta of primitive accumulation. […] If money, according to Angier, 'comes into the world with a congenital blood stain on one cheek,' capital comes dripping from head to foot, from every pore, with blood and dirt." Marx, *Capital*. Volume I Chapter XXXI.

8. Marx, *Poverty of Philosophy*. Chapter II Section I (*Oeuvres* Tome I, 80).

9. Robinson, 323.

10. Ibid., 19.

11. See Marx's letter to V.I. Zasulich, March 8, 1881, where he says explicitly that "The historical inevitability" (of the process of the genesis of capitalism discussed in his *Capital*) is expressly limited to the countries of Western Europe. (Marx and Engels, *Selected Correspondence*, 339)

12. Su, 58.

The Relevance of the Critique of Eurocentrism for the Twenty First Century World Order

THERE are always two aspects to the anti-Eurocentric position. On the one hand the task is to lay bare the *true* Eurocentrism which the system tries to hide. From this angle, it is important to affirm that the present day order is still a pyramid with, at its apex, the Euro-American white world. It has co-opted certain "honorary Aryans," but in a clearly subordinate role. Through its institutions, G7(8), the Organisation for Economic Co-operation and Development (OECD) and NATO, it makes all the meaningful decisions. It uses the Bretton Woods institutions—the IMF, World Bank, and the latest addition to its weaponry, the WTO—to enforce its economic dogmas. It pumps out ideology and culture into all corners of the globe. The system projects a veneer of inclusivity—for example, in the discourse that the growth generated by globalisation will create a larger "cake" for all to share—but its doctrine is explicit that this supposed growth is conditional on subordinating everything to the reproduction of capital, which in substance means the expanded reproduction of capital at the core. A well-coordinated military apparatus is on hand to intervene in any situation where the economic and ideological levers are judged inadequate. This is the reality. At the same time, we still have the essential task of critiquing the Eurocentrist *lie*, the dominant system of ideas which denies the creativity and leading role of those who are excluded or marginalised from official history—both the role which non-European peoples have always played in the past, and the contemporary role which the most excluded can play in rescuing humanity from its current crisis.

The Eurocentric power structure—together with the ideology which serves to promote, and also partly to conceal and mystify it—has certain abiding features, and also assumes new forms in each period. Its present form is the hegemonic discourse, aspiring to siphon into itself all available space for debate, permitting no contestation: a fatalistic, deterministic vision of something called globalisation, a fatality which is apparently just "there," independent of human will, with the effect that people can only conform or perish—it is presumably just an accident that it happens to consolidate and promote the existing dominant class interests! The ruling discourse scarcely accepts that anyone *could* question it but, if they did, they would be branded a primitive, a pathetic historical relic, a lunatic, a dangerous misleader of development into blind alleys. Again, unilinear thinking and Eurocentrism go hand in hand.

The force which challenges all this, the current to which we have been referring throughout this book, is still present: the radical forces who *are* determined to make their own history. The centre of this trend is still the South, the superexploited periphery of the global capitalist system. Its most advanced form is the Marxist forces which openly refuse the system's logic; its more diffuse form is the wider mass movement. The fundamental point is therefore still the same: we need the anti-Eurocentric perspective in order to appreciate that there *are* these creative forces, and that the dominant interests do not have everything their own way.

The Eurocentric perspective within the left was falsely optimistic in the sense of failing to sense the resilience or adaptability of the oppressor system, based upon its ability to intensify the exploitation of the periphery while defusing class struggle within the core. And this false optimism naturally (and quite suddenly, as is the way with tipping-points) tipped over into its opposite, an unjustified pessimism and liquidation. The reason is quite simply that the real basis for optimism was never perceived: that the excluded had never stopped fighting, and that heightened exploitation could only intensify their resistance. This remains the fundamental strategic reality, but in a tactical sense the system has adapted itself in ways which can, on the surface, be quite confusing. For this reason, the critical perspective is in many ways even more needed today than it was when this research was initially conducted, at the time when the Cold War was drawing to a close.

While the Cold War still reigned, the ruling interests made much play of attacking communism. Of course, they used the term in a distorted way, and additional confusion was spread by the Soviet system which was not really communist at all and understandably turned many people off. Nevertheless, capitalism was at least open about fighting communism; this had the result that the masses suffering under imperialism tended to gravitate towards communist leadership. Moreover, the manner in which imperialism ruled the periphery was exclusively top-down, typically through local henchmen who ran militaristic dictatorships with little pretence even of democratic trappings. It therefore had little scope for engaging with social movements in order to *stop* them moving to the left.

In the more recent period, the notion of the "end of history" has been employed to "freeze out" communism by denying its existence. At the same time, the ruling order has experimented with important ways of operating *within* the social movement. It is now able to co-opt not just the elites as before, but also parts of the mass movement. Employing a discourse of "governance" and "civil society," it disburses pittances of aid to subservient campaigns or pressure groups, baptising them as NGOs and community-based organisations. This serves a dual purpose:

firstly, to erect a barrier between the political left and the wider movement; secondly, to use people's grassroots survival strategies—through such mechanisms as micro-credit—to generate more value for accumulation, and as low-cost means of social control.

In these ways, the real lines of demarcation and the reality of dominance have been somewhat obscured. But two issues must be made clear. First of all, there is absolutely no doubt that beneath the surface the fundamental contradictions are stronger than ever: all the adaptations of global capitalism are essentially means of intensifying exploitation, and the surface forms which may for a time appear to attenuate that exploitation are wholly illusory. Secondly, these surface forms—the more indirect and diffuse forms of dominance which undoubtedly did help to consolidate global capitalism for a while following the Cold War's end—are increasingly wearing thin. This is the reason why the system suddenly engaged, in the last years of the 1990s, in a decisive shift into repression and militarism.

Our purpose in this chapter is to address *contemporary* realities, and "contemporary" must be understood in a dual sense. The general sense refers to the whole period associated with the end of the Cold War, the second and more precise sense refers to the sub-phase beginning around 1997. Marxist forces must adapt themselves to this rapidly-evolving reality, which is why theoretical tools such as a critique of Eurocentrism are so important. The consolidation of the 1980s and the crisis of the 2000s are part of the same phenomenon, simply because that consolidation was premised on heightened exploitation, and a heightened crisis was always the inevitable result. But it is impossible to properly understand the crisis without understanding the consolidation which preceded it. We therefore need to consider the characteristics of this complex period.

Let us first recapitulate some of the key perspectives which have been developed in this book. The point about the critique of Eurocentrism is certainly not to undermine the significance of class. The key issue is still and has always been that the system is founded on the exploitation of those who perform labour. The point is that you need to delve below the surface in order to appreciate the *reality* of that exploitation, of who performs the labour, and under what conditions. Capitalism has developed a dualism within the labouring masses, with some groups more exploited than others. If we were to view this in a purely economic sense, it might seem to be a difference in *degree*. But the dialectical aspect of Marxism is that, while in one sense we say that things are *based in* economics, in another sense the superstructure (ideas, culture, politics) plays the key role, both in the *maintenance and adaptation* of systems, and in *challenging* them. Considering this wider context, the issue in dualism is in fact not merely the degree of exploitation, because the political, ideological, cultural dimension deprives the super-oppressed group of their human rights.

When we describe capitalism as a *system* we mean that it has acquired a momentum of its own, one which is not predetermined and not entirely predictable. It is a product of human social development which has got out of control and threatens to devour the human species which made it. The fruits of people's labour turn into a force which oppresses and limits them. This takes the form not just of capital itself, but of ideological and cultural structures. The latter in some sense reflect reality, but in a distorted way. With racism, the fundamental basis is not real, inasmuch as "race" itself has no sense as a scientific category; but the oppressive categories are real in terms of deeply rooted social practices and attitudes. We can call this the "structural factor" within capitalism. Capitalists themselves do not fully control these processes, though they manipulate them to their own advantage. In this sense, conspiracy theories have their place, but we should beware of exaggerating their scope. It is actually the extreme right which uses conspiracy theories to cover up the structural element in capitalism. For this reason the simplistic view of racism as merely a conspiracy to divide the working class is dangerously wrong, precisely because it makes an abstraction of the structural dimension, which is crucial.

The natural vocation of the anti-capitalist movement *should* be that its orientation predominantly reflect the standpoint of the most marginalised and oppressed stratum. However, there are important reasons why this does not happen automatically. Because of structurally-embedded social practices, the default position is one where the movement's public face tends to be the one which is relatively *less* marginalised from the seat of power—the white, male aspect. This will remain the default position until challenged, and insofar as it is *not* challenged, the effect of dualism will eventually come back to haunt the white male working class, simply because the most savage forms of exploitation, originally meted out against the most vulnerable, will sooner or later be used against them. The recent phase of capitalism has found new ways to explore these possibilities. The general expression of these new approaches is the so-called "new management systems," the informalisation and "flexibilisation" of labour, which provided one basis for the consolidation in the 1980s. This partly signifies that the determinants of the exploitation of the most oppressed segments, which were not adequately challenged by the majority movement, are suddenly foisted upon the wider working class who wake up to the truth when it is too late. The labour of women and of groups oppressed through racial determinants was always treated as informal and flexible; now all workers are vulnerable to being treated the same way. But the fact that certain determinants of exploitation have "spread" to a wider group does not signify a weakening of dualism, quite the contrary; it has instead been shifted into new dimensions, and in fact accentuated. The global industrial economy is now organised through production chains, bound together by subcontracting relationships. The advanced capitalist core seeks to monopolise high technology at the top of the chain, while exporting risk, uncertainty and misery to the lower levels of the chain, where the marginalised segment of workers lead a precarious existence fulfilling labour-intensive assembly tasks. **The technology which could be used to reduce labour is thus in fact increasing it.** Through the "new public management" and other tactics, these systems also become the pattern for all economic sectors, including the service sector where many of the most heavily exploited are concentrated. And alongside all this there are the unemployed who are forced to work in the most informal and menial way.

The essential issues of racism which we identified in our historical study are still at work, only in new, and possibly expanded ways. Racism has always taken two interdependent forms, assimilation and exclusion. The "globalisation" discourse is the contemporary form of the assimilationist aspect, which at first sight appears to predominate: anyone who totally internalises and uncritically articulates the discourse can seemingly gain acceptance. But, as with all forms of assimilation, this is a kind of "equality" where the very act of fulfilling its requirements is a demonstration of your inferiority! Your acceptance must be slavish, and that brands you as a slave. Moreover, the promise of equality is obviously false. Only a very small minority can enjoy the "benefits" of such inclusion/co-optation. The rest must parrot the discourse *without* enjoying its fruits; or, if they question it, the full weight of the exclusionary aspect then falls upon them, in the shape of outright repression.

Alongside the co-optation of selected segments in selected regions of the South into the accumulation process of globalised capital, the relative poverty of the masses continues to get worse—it cannot be otherwise if Southern capital frantically competes for the benefits of an export promotion model essentially premised on cheap labour. One of the most important effects of this increasing poverty is migration. As capital becomes ever more mobile, the boundaries of the mobility of labour are more and more savagely policed. These boundaries reflect the unequal value of life in core and periphery, which must at all costs be maintained. Nevertheless, their concrete function is not actually to *stop* migration, but to ensure that when it happens (as it inevitably does), the oppressed group remains in servitude. The North does not actually want to exclude migrants *from* its frontiers, it wants to exclude them *within* its frontiers. In the process, global capitalism has created a new super-marginalised group with no status, "illegal" workers, people without papers, maintained in a precarious status so that the system can superexploit them. This is the most important contemporary form of the issues of dualism and exclusion addressed in this book. Against this social and economic background, we should now consider the reasons for the new political and military situation.

For a while, from the 1980s on, the system could adapt itself, and rule partly through disguised, indirect methods. For many years before that, people across the world had been disgusted by the repressive, dictatorial forms of neo-colonial rule which characterised the Cold War. Therefore, a mass movement for democratisation developed in many countries. Of course, imperialism was the real puppet-master of the old repressive setups, and should have been the *target* of democratisation movements. However, imperialism managed to reposition itself by infiltrating this movement, presenting itself as a champion of "good governance" against corruption, and creating new, pseudo-democratic forms of indirect rule which were more efficient than the old dictatorships. As part of this change, the new agenda of reduced trade barriers claims to open up opportunity: international capitalism suddenly woke up to the fact that it could accede to the long-term demand of the Southern bourgeoisie, for access for their exports to Northern markets—because the new system of production chains provides a great mechanism to recoup the profit generated by cheap Southern labour in manufacturing these products. But the weaknesses in this setup were soon exposed. Although some segments of the elite could be co-opted in this way, their "integration" only accentuates the relative poverty of those marginalised by globalisation. Moreover, the semblance of opportunity even for the capitalists of the South is hard to maintain. For example, the "intellectual property" issue is used rigidly to police the core's monopoly of knowledge. Even the elites may become disgruntled, and although there is of course no chance that they could *lead* anti-imperialist struggles, the possibility certainly surfaces of assembling broad coalitions under working-class leadership.

With the indirect control mechanisms becoming increasingly unreliable, international capitalism took a fateful step at the close of the 1990s, towards a total strategy of open aggression, militarisation, and war. As with other developments of capitalism, this took the immediate form of a conspiracy, in this case on the part of the clique figure-headed by George W. Bush; but at a deeper level it expresses profound objective tendencies in capitalism which have continued and even intensified post-Bush. The militaristic-repressive option is primarily directed at the recalcitrant aspect of the mass movements and national movements, and more specifically against revolutionary forces. It was a pre-emptive move: a mass revolt did not yet exist, but the system was positioning itself in anticipation of this. The purpose of adopting "terrorism" as a slogan for this new phase is to fight the radical movement, while continuing to deny that it exists. Undoubtedly, this policy shift will produce the result it fears—heightened struggle. However, it poses new, complex tasks for the Marxist forces, and here again issues addressed in the critique of Eurocentrism are centrally relevant.

In practice, it seems likely that the core of resistance will be Maoism. The basic Maoist position, derived from the Chinese stance against revisionism, was that imperialism will never give up power without defending its interests by violence. The CPC understood this because, being part of the oppressed periphery, it possessed first hand knowledge of how conflict, temporarily eliminated in the Euro-Atlantic world by the Cold War stabilisation, was exported to the South. The most recent situation, writing in the 2010s, amply confirms what Maoism has always maintained: imperialism now turns the clock back to a situation of extreme militarism directed against the masses worldwide. It will have to be seen whether the subjective forces are able to respond to this challenge. The whole key will be the relationship between the organised radical contingent and the wider movement. The generalised, endemic level of struggle never ceases, and it still very strongly encompasses the kind of forces we have been speaking of in this book: those marginalised not only just through racist oppression but in other, often superposed ways, particularly gender, and all the forms of super-exclusion characteristic of the globalisation era—informality, various forms of indentured service, lack of status, lack of papers. Here, too, the Maoist tradition fully retains its relevance: it always critiqued the labour movement tendency to perceive only those segments of the working population who fall under the limelight of official recognition.

The creativity of the wider mass movement can supply resources not just for the struggle against the current order, but for the building of a new one: popular initiative, grassroots innovation in production, indigenous know-how in agriculture—all the ways of generating an endogenous value which does not depend on the Northern-dominated circuits of global capital. This approach is also relevant from an organisational angle. The founders of Marxism were always respectful towards the forms generated by the actual struggle, using them to reinvigorate the organised structures—for example, Marx with the Paris Commune, Lenin with the workers' councils (soviets). We only need to see that the most creative force generating new organisational forms today are the superexploited masses: women's organisations, indigenous movements, new forms of trade unionism, etc. Besides the mass movement, there are many trends among different classes and strata which may seem to challenge dominant agendas in certain respects at certain times, which still include forms of nationalism. How to assess these forces? There is a very clear answer to this problem, which was spelled out in Lenin's important book *Left-Wing Communism, an Infantile Disorder*, and is still exactly as relevant as when he first advanced it: such trends are either progressive or reactionary according to circumstances, and nothing can replace a concrete analysis of the precise conditions in a particular country, and of the precise juncture within the historical progression of the world movement.

The issues addressed in relation to Eurocentrism have a major role in making such judgments. One of the key issues in our historiography was to consider the adaptation of Marxism to take account of the reality of non-European cultures; this must be approached in a context highly specific to today's contradictions. One of the main ways capitalism has survived has been by capturing rebellion from within, emphasising co-optable forms, or even inventing them where they do not exist. With respect to the issue of culture, the dominant order has adapted in a complex way. Importantly, it has learned how to infiltrate *contradictory* trends, which seem to wage a shadow-war against one another, but with ruling interest pulling the strings. A striking example lies in the system's way of relating to multiculturalism and fundamentalism. One of the remarkable adaptations of ruling ideology is to have *itself* parasitised the critique of Eurocentrism, side-tracking it into a "postmodern" form. Whereas the globalisation discourse is frankly the same as the old unilinear developmental theories, the postmodern approach aims to colonise the critique *against* that theory, replacing the old assimilationist, homogenising discourse with one emphasising cultural relativism and the separateness of cultures—with the result that it would be impossible to make *generalisations* about exploitation and the resistance to it. This is the opposite to the way the term Eurocentrism has been used in our book: our historiography has highlighted a trend towards unity, within a coherent radical political movement, while emphasising that this unity will be totally false if it is premised upon perpetuating the dominance of the cultural system forged by colonialism. The radical anti-Eurocentric movement will remain *diverse*, closely integrated with the social characteristics, the natural world, and the traditions of each country and region, and in this sense it is important that the homogenising tendency of globalism will not be replaced by any other homogenisation. But on this basis, the Marxist aspiration towards internationalism will fully continue to apply: we *can* generalise about exploitation and aspire to unify the current of resistance against it. The creation of a phoney war between assimilationism and postmodern multiculturalism is therefore one aspect of adaptation in the capitalist superstructure. But parallel to this, multiculturalism erects also another phoney war, enlisting a phenomenon seeming to stand outside and oppose both these trends: fundamentalism. Fundamentalism now plays a big role in supplying phoney targets for the ultra-militaristic turn. We could say that, in conducting this adaptation, the system is, in a sense, *parasitical on the symptoms of its own decay*.

As Marx understood, the basis of alienation under capitalism is that everything becomes commodified. Relations of people to one another, and between people and nature, are reduced to commodity relations. This undermines the spirituality which is inherent in humanity, the sense of being one with the natural world, as well as the sense of unity with the products of one's own labour. Social relations within the core are already totally screwed up by this alienation, but what is worse is that the system—increasingly, in the era of "globalisation"—foists this alienation aggressively upon the rest of the world. Only, in this case, the system does not even confer the "development" it promises: the periphery gets to experience the alienation associated with commodification without enjoying the commodities themselves! On this basis there inevitably develops a diffuse movement of disillusionment with the soullessness of the current order, and such currents quite naturally find a certain point of reference in the moral and spiritual dimensions of traditional culture. In substance, this should be a movement *against* capitalism, but the system's adaptation has been to convert this alienation into distorted forms which bolster its own power, thereby artificially delaying its demise. The headquarters of this distorted tendency is found in the weird fundamentalist movements centred in the USA, which acquired a certain ascendancy under the presidency of George W. Bush. Here the sophistications of postmodernism are cast aside, turning the clock back beyond the cold rationalism of the Enlightenment to a more primitive, twisted form of obscurantism reminiscent of the witch-hunts and Inquisitions of decayed European feudalism. At an international level, it reverts to the heavily normative, crusading vision characteristic of atavistic Eurocentrism. Indeed, it openly refers back to the old crusades. Just as the old racists presented world history as a clash between so-called "races," history is now pushed into the mould of a clash between rival fundamentalisms. By manufacturing an enemy in its own mirror image, imperialism seeks to divert oppositional currents into similarly fundamentalist forms, thereby removing them from the leadership of the left.

This presents a difficult challenge. Here we see what is perhaps the most important single contribution which can be made by the issues addressed in this book to the contemporary world. The historic anti-Eurocentric current had begun to hint at a way of making Marxism relevant to issues not just of cultural tradition in the oppressed nations, but more broadly of the collapse of human beings' relations with each other and with nature—of the spiritual dimension of the human experience under conditions of rampant global capitalism. Because mainstream Marxism never explored the potential of that insight, it was left to the ruling order to do so in a distorted way, and in its own interest. But that can be challenged. The system is now entering a profound crisis, and it is important to be clear that the repressive and ultra-reactionary trend is **not** the outcome of a clever conspiracy, but rather of desperation—this is the positive aspect. However, the negative side is that the crisis is one which threatens to drag humanity down with it: capitalism is not just *capable* (in an instrumental sense) of sacrificing the future of humanity as a whole to the short-term prolongation of the capitalist mode of production, it is set on a course where it is objectively *bound* to do so.

Our book has taken the form of a historiography, which naturally seems to relate to the past, but its point is of course to see how, on the basis of an understanding of existing trends, we can create the future. The notion of a "historiography of the future" is contradictory in a dialectical sense, but not absurd: simply, we must understand that it describes a development which is just a possibility, not a certainty. Capitalism *could* destroy the legacy of human history, or it could be prevented from doing so. Disorder can be expected to grow, and the established norms of capitalist society weaken. As these bonds loosen, new phenomena arise. Some of these emergent things are good and encouraging: popular survival strategies which hold within them the seeds of a new social order. Others are highly dangerous and chaotic. The way the system looks to be going at present seems designed to suppress the creative aspects and give free rein to all the unhealthy manifestations of a decaying order.

Declining capitalism seems locked in a death-embrace with the symptoms of its own decay. While going to its own grave, it is determined to drag humanity down with it. To reverse this tendency is the task now facing the left. If capitalism prides itself on having manoeuvered the left into a place where it is hard to engage with these issues, it could do so only because of the left's internal weakness.

The point of this book is that Marxism has a potential much larger than what has been realised so far in its conventional organised forms; it is now indispensible to surpass these limitations. Where the system marginalises the periphery, the excluded, we must place them in the centre of the picture. There is a bifurcation of history. We cannot predict the exact way in which a potentially revolutionary situation will arise. It will emerge out of a situation of complexity, and at some point will tip over from semi-passive suffering into revolt. This is as far as our "future historiography" can go. It is not certain that the radical forces will be able to seize this chance and rescue humanity. But, if armed with a historical understanding which identifies the most intensely oppressed and the most creative forces, it will indeed be equipped to rise to the challenge.

Bibliography

Abraham, Kinfe. *From Race to Class*. London: Grassroots, 1982.

Amin, Samir. "Der Marxismus in Asien und Afrika." *Kommune: Forum für Politik, Ökonomie, Kultur* 1:4 (April 1983), 33–52.

Amin, Samir. *La Loi de la valeur et le matérialisme historique*. Paris: Minuit, 1977.

Anderson, Kevin. *Marx at the Margins: On Nationalism, Ethnicity and Non-Western Societies*. Chicago: University of Chicago Press, 2010.

Armah, Ayi Kwei. "Masks and Marx: The Marxist ethos vis a vis African Revolutionary Theory and Praxis." In *Présence Africaine* 131:3 (1984): 35–65.

Azanian People's Organisation (AZAPO) *Conference Issue* (February 1983).

Baku: Congress of the Peoples of the East. London: New Park Publications, 1977.

Banerjee, Sumanta. *India's Simmering Revolution*. London: Zed, 1984.

Bashear, Suliman. *Communism in the Arab East*. London: Ithaca Press, 1980.

Bennigson, A. "Sultan Galiev: The USSR and the Colonial Revolution." In *The Middle East in Transition* (W.Z. Laqeur, ed.). London: Routledge & Kegan Paul, 1958.

Campbell, Alexander. *It's Your Empire*. London: Left Book Club, 1945.

Cesaire, Aimé. *Discourse on Colonialism*. London: Monthly Review Press, 1972.

Communist Party of Britain (Marxist-Leninist). *The British Working Class and its Party*. London: self-published, 1971.

Communist Party of China. *The Polemic on the General Line of the International Communist Movement*. Peking: Foreign Language Press, 1965.

Communist Party of Great Britain. *The Colonies: The Way Forward—A Memorandum issued by the Executive Committee of the CP*. London: self-published, 1944.

Communist Party of Great Britain. *Political Economy: Marxist Study Courses*. Chicago: Banner Press, 1976.

Cummins, Ian. *Marx, Engels and the National Movements*. London: Croome Helm, 1980.

Curtin, Philip D. *The Image of Africa: British Ideas and Action 1780–1850*. London: Macmillan, 1965.

Curtin, Philip D. *Imperialism: Documentary History of Western Civilization*. London: Macmillan, 1972.

Darwin, Charles. *The Voyage of the Beagle*. London: Everyman, 1959.

Davis, Horace B. *Nationalism and Socialism: Marxist and Labour Theories of Nationalism to 1917*. New York: Monthly Review Press, 1967.

Dia, Mamadou. *Dialogue des Nations*. Alger: Société Nationale d'Edition et de Diffusion, 1980.

Dimitrov, Georgi. *For the Unity of the Working Class against Fascism*. London: Red Star Press, 1973.

Diop, Cheikh Anta. *L'Afrique noire précoloniale— étude comparée des systèmes politiques et sociaux de l'Europe et de l'Afrique noire, de l'antiquité à la formation des états modernes*. Paris: Présence africaine, 1960.

Du Bois, W.E.B. *The Suppression of the African Slave-trade to the United States of America 1638–1870*. New York: Russell and Russell, 1965.

Dühring, Eugen. *Cursus der National- und Socialoekonomie*. Berlin: Theobald Grieber, 1873.

Dutt, R. Palme. *World Politics 1918–1936*. London: Gollancz, 1936.

Engels, Friedrich. *Anti-Dühring*. Moscow: Progress Publishers, 1969.

Fanon, Frantz. *The Wretched of the Earth*. London: Penguin, 1967.

Fei Xiatong. *Towards a People's Anthropology*. Peking: New World Press, 1981.

Feuerbach, Ludwig. *The Essence of Christianity*. New York: Harper & Row, 1957.

Field, H. John. *Towards a Program of Imperial Life: The British Empire at the turn of the Century*. Oxford: Clio Press, 1982.

Forum for Marxist-Leninist Struggle. *The National Liberation Movement Today as Seen by Dutt, Krushchev and Others*. London: Forum for Marxist-Leninist Struggle, 1964.

Front culturel sénégalais. *Lamine Senghor: Vie et Oeuvre*, Senegal: self-published, 1979.

Fryer, Peter. *Staying Power: the History of Black People in Britain*. London: Pluto, 1984.

Gobineau, Arthur. *Essai sur l'inégalité des races humaines*, Volume 1. Paris: Firmin-Didot, 191? (1854)

Godelier, Maurice. Preface to *Marx, Engels, Lénine sur les Sociétés précapitalistes: Textes choisies*, (eds. Sociales pour Centre d'Etudes et de Récherches marxistes). Paris: Editions sociales, 1973.

Goonatilake, Susantha. *Crippled Minds: An Exploration into Colonial Culture*. New Delhi: Vikas Publishing House, 1982.

Haupt, George. "Les marxistes face à la question nationale." In *Les marxistes et la question nationale 1848–1914*, (George Haupt, et al., eds.). Paris: Maspero, 1974.

Hayes, Paul M. *Fascism*. London: G. Allen and Unwin, 1973.

Huttenback, Robert A. *Racism and Empire: White Settlers and Coloured Immigrants in the British Self-governing colonies 1830–1910*. Ithaca: Cornell University Press, 1976.

L'Impérialisme Aujourd'hui: Traité sur l'Impérialisme, Stade suprême du capitalisme. Paris: Editions du Centenaire, 1976.

James, C.L.R. *The Black Jacobins: Toussaint L'Ouverture and the San Domingo Revolution (New Edition)*. London: Allison and Busby, 1980.

Jordan, Winthrop D. *White Over Black: American Attitudes toward the Negro 1550–1812*. Chapel Hill: University of North Carolina Press, 1968.

Jurquet, Jacques. *Révolution nationale algérienne et le Parti Communiste français*, Volume II. Paris: Editions du Centenaire, 1974.

Knox, Robert. *The Races of Man (2nd Edition)*. London: Henry Renshaw, 1862.

Leith, C.K. *World Minerals and World Politics*. New York: Kennicat Press, 1970.

Lenin, V.I. *Collected Works*, Volume 30. Moscow: Progress Publishers, 1974.

Lenin, V.I. *Collected Works*, Volume 33. Moscow: Progress Publishers, 1973.

Lenin, V.I. *Collected Works*, Volume 38. Moscow: Progress Publishers, 1976.

Lenin, V.I. *Imperialism, the Highest stage of Capitalism*. Peking: Foreign Language Press, 1970.

Lenin, V.I. *Marx-Engels-Marxism*. Peking: Foreign Language Press, 1978.

Lenin, V.I. *Selected Works*, Volume 3. Moscow: Progress, 1971.

Leontiev, A. *Political Economy: A Beginner's Course*. San Francisco: Proletarian Publishers, 1974.

Lin Biao. *Long Live the Victory of People's War!* Peking: Foreign Language Press, 1967.

Lotta, Raymond and Frank Shannon. *America in Decline*, Volume 1. Chicago: Banner Press, 1984.

Luxemburg, Rosa. *The Accumulation of Capital: An Anti-Critique*. New York: Monthly Review Press, 1972.

Malthus, Thomas Robert. *An Essay on Population*. London: Everyman, 1958.

Mannoni, Octave. *Prospero and Caliban: the Psychology of Colonisation*. London: Methuen, 1956.

Mao Zedong. *Statement by Comrade Mao Tse Tung, Chairman of the Central Committee of the Communist Party of China, in Support of the Afro-American Struggle against violent repression*. Peking: Foreign Language Press, 1968.

Mao Zedong. *Statement Calling on the People of the World to Unite to Oppose Racial Discrimination by US Imperialism and Support the American Negroes in their Struggle against Racial Discrimination*. Peking: Foreign Language Press, 1964.

Marx, Karl. *Capital*, Volume I. London: Lawrence & Wishart, 2003.

Marx, Karl. *The Ethnological Notebooks of Karl Marx (2nd Edition)*. (Transcribed and edited by L. Krader.) Assen: Van Gorcum & Co., 1974.

Marx, Karl. *Notes on Indian History*. Moscow: Foreign Languages Publishing House, 1960.

Marx, Karl. *Oeuvres: Economie*, Tome II. Paris: Gallimard, 1968.

Marx, Karl. *On China: Articles from the New York Daily Tribune 1853–60*. London: Lawrence and Wishart, 1968.

Marx, Karl. *The Poverty of Philosophy*. New York: International Publishers, 1975.

Marx, Karl. *Secret Diplomatic History of the Eighteenth Century.* (Edited by Eleanor Marx Aveling.) London: Swan Sonnenschein & Co., 1899.

Marx, Karl and Friedrich Engels. *The Communist Manifesto.* Peking: Foreign Language Press, 1970.

Marx, Karl and Friedrich Engels. *Ireland and the Irish Question.* Moscow: Progress Publishers, 1971.

Marx, Karl and Friedrich Engels. *Marx and Engels: Selected Works.* Moscow: Progress Publishers, 1969–1970.

Marx, Karl and Friedrich Engels. *On Colonialism (4th Edition).* Moscow: Progress Publishers, 1968.

Marx, Karl and Friedrich Engels. *Selected Correspondence (2nd Revised Edition).* Moscow: Progress Publishers, 1965.

Maser, Werner. *Hitler's Mein Kampf: An Analysis.* London: Faber and Faber, 1970.

McCreery, M. *The Way Forward: The Need to Establish a Communist Party in England, Scotland, Wales.* London: the Committee to Defeat Revisionism for Communist Unity, 1964.

Meisner, Maurice. *Li Ta-chao and the Origins of Chinese Marxism.* New York: Atheneum, 1970.

Moore, Carlos. *Were Marx and Engels White Racists?* Chicago: Institute of Positive Education, 1972.

Morgan, Lewis H. *Ancient Society or Researches in the Lines of Human Progress from Savagery through Barbarism to Civilisation.* Chicago: Charles H. Kerr & Co., 1908.

Mosses, George L. *Toward the Final Solution: A History of European Racism.* London: Dent & Sons, 1978.

N'Dumbe III, A Kum'a. *Hitler Voulait l'Afrique.* Paris: l'Harmattan, 1980.

Nolte, Ernst. "The Problem of Fascism in Recent Scholarship." In *Re-appraisals of Fascism* (H.J. Turner, ed.), New York: New Viewpoints, 1975.

Nolte, Ernst. *Three Faces of Fascism*. New York: Mentor, 1969.

October I (1980s).

Pearce, Roy Harvey. *The Savages of America*. Baltimore: John Hopkins University Press, 1965.

Ranger, Terrence O. *Revolt in Southern Rhodesia*. Evanston: Northwestern University Press, 1967.

Ridley, H. *Images of Imperial Rule*. London: Croome Helm, 1983.

Robinson, C.J. *Black Marxism*. London: Zed Books, 1983.

Rodney, Walter. *How Europe Underdeveloped Africa*. London: Bogle l'Overture Publications, 1972.

Rosdolsky, Roman. "Friedrich Engels u. das Problem der 'geschichtslosen Völker.'" In *Archiv für Sozialgeschichte*: 4 (1964).

Rostow, W.W. *The Stages of Economic Growth: A Non-Communist Manifesto*. Cambridge: Cambridge University Press, 1960.

Schneefuss, W. *Gefahrenzonen des Britischen Weltreiches*. Leipzig: Wilhelm Goldmann Verlag, 1938.

Sigrist, C. "Akephale politische Systeme und Nationale Befreiung." In *Traditionale Gesellschaften und europäischer Kolonialismus* (J.H. Grevemeyer, ed.). Frankfurt-am-Main: Syndikat, 1981.

Snowden, F.M. *Before Colour Prejudice: the Ancient View of Blacks*. Cambridge: Harvard University Press, 1983.

Spengler, Oswald. *The Decline of the West: Form and Activity*. London: G. Allen and Unwin, 1926.

Stalin, J.V. *Economic Problems of Socialism in the USSR*. Peking: Foreign Language Press, 1972.

Stalin, J.V. *Works*, Volume 3. London: Red Star Press, 1975.

Stalin, J.V. *Works*, Volume 4. London: Red Star Press, 1975.

Su Shaozhi, et,al. *Marxism in China*. London: Spokesman Books, 1983.

Szentes, Tamas. "The Main Theoretical Questions of 'Underdevelopment'." In *Theory and Practice of Development in the Third World* (J. Nyilas, ed.). Leyden: A.W. Sijthoff for Akademie Kiado Budapest, 1977.

Taharka, Sundiata. *Black Manhood (Revised Edition)*. Washington: University Press of America, 1979.

Theses, Resolutions and Manifestos of the First Four Congresses of the Third International. London: Ink Links and Humanities Press, 1980.

Ulyanovsky, R.A. (editor). *The Comintern and the East*. Moscow: Progress Publishers, 1979.

de Vattel, Emer. *The Law of Nations (Washington Edition, 1916)*. In *Imperialism* (P.D. Curtin, ed.), London: Macmillan, 1972.

Vindex. *Cecil Rhodes: His Political Life and Speeches 1881–1900*. London: Chapman Hall Ltd, 1900.

Wood, John Cunningham. *British Economists and the Empire*. London: Croome Helm, 1983.

Yeats, W.B. *Collected Poems*. London: Macmillan, 1963.

About the Author

Robert Biel teaches political ecology at University College London and is the author of *The New Imperialism* and *The Entropy of Capitalism*. He researches systems theory and conducts a wide-ranging practical programme on urban agriculture.

What People Are Saying

In a provocative and compelling analysis, Robert Biel enters into the global efforts at Marxist renewal by taking, straight-on, one of the major deficiencies in the Marxist tradition: Eurocentrism. This work is striking in its willingness to critically re-examine multiple currents in Marxism thereby helping the reader to appreciate major factors that have led to a stagnation within the larger left of the Global North. Biel challenges not only Eurocentrism but the corresponding economic determinism that has frequently limited the scope and reach of radical left social movements. I found myself thinking about the famous phrase, attributed to Italian Marxist Antonio Gramsci, to the effect that "...the truth is always revolutionary." To which I would add, no matter how challenging it may be to address it.

Bill Fletcher, Jr., co-author of <u>Solidarity Divided</u>*; syndicated columnist*

A long overdue second appearance as it was singularly the most outstanding contribution in the checkered history of the anti-revisionist movement in Britain. It was an exciting, fertile exploration to developing the need to make concrete and relevant the general theses adopted in the 1960s. One aspect that provided disastrously correct was that the effect of the Eurocentric outlook upon those young Maoist organisations was that when the time came to criticise dogmatic and sectarian errors, this was often done not from a revolutionary standpoint but from a rightist and liquidationist one.

Sam Richards, Encyclopedia of Anti-Revisionism Online

Robert Biel's *Eurocentrism and the Communist Movement* is a conscientious and well-researched effort to present Eurocentrism as a colonial, racist, and social-chauvinist mentality and phenomenon. It decries this problem as having overvalued European developments and influence under the rubric of "progress," depreciated the history and dynamic of the oppressed peoples and nations, subordinated their revolutionary role and aspirations to the European states and industrial proletariat, and in effect favoured colonialism and the slave trade and the entire train of consequences up to neocolonialism and neoliberalism.

Biel points out that the imperialist powers have been able to maintain relative unity and overcome crisis after crisis since World War II by escalating the exploitation and oppression of the peoples of the Third World. The revolutionary struggle of the oppressed peoples and nations is therefore of decisive importance in bringing down the imperialist system. This is an important point to keep in mind, especially at this time when the policy of neoliberal globalisation has brought about great social devastation mainly at the expense of the peoples and nations of Asia, Africa, and Latin America.

The book highlights and underscores what it repeatedly calls "unilinear" thinking in the communist movement about stages of social development and "limitations" of the great communist thinkers and leaders in combatting Eurocentrism. In this regard, it invites debate on the validity and proportionality of the criticisms, especially as these pertain to the period prior to the rise of modern revisionism and Soviet social-imperialism which joined the neocolonial game and coined the "non-capitalist path of development" for the Third World. At any rate, Biel acknowledges the fact that from period to period the theory and practice of Marxism-Leninism up to Maoism have increasingly taken into account the decisive importance and revolutionary role of the oppressed peoples and nations of Asia, Africa, and Latin America.

Marx pointed out and condemned the extreme exploitation of peoples through colonialism and slavery in the primitive accumulation of capital and in the further development of capitalism. Lenin fought against Kautsky's theory of ultra-imperialism and the social-chauvinist and colonialist position of the Second International. Lenin and Stalin actually moved the world proletarian revolution to the East and led the liberation of the Russia-dominated nationalities. The Third International caused the establishment of communist parties and promoted the revolutionary movements in the East. Mao moved the world revolution further to the East, led the revolutionary cause of national liberation, people's democracy, and socialism and fought modern revisionism and Soviet social imperialism. In my view, Marxism-Leninism-Maoism stands today as a coherent, resolute and militant response to the escalation of oppression and exploitation of the peoples of Asia, Africa, and Latin America.

Robert Biel upholds the national and social aspirations of the broad masses of the people against imperialism and all reaction and criticizes those who misuse the critique of Eurocentrism to deny or oppose the revolutionary class struggles of the proletariat and peasants. He gives special praise to Samir Amin for his dependency theory which points to the impoverishment of the people in the periphery of underdeveloped states as a result of the flow of resources to the core of wealthy states. He appreciates highly the African anti-colonial and anti-imperialist theorists like Amilcar Cabral and the African-American Marxists like W.E.B. Dubois and Robert Williams who fought the continuing extreme oppression and exploitation of African-Americans. He gives some attention to the Maoist communist parties and peoples fighting for national liberation and democracy in the Philippines, India, Nepal, Peru, and elsewhere.

Professor José María Sison,
chairperson of the International Coordinating Committee,
International League of Peoples' Struggle

ALSO FROM KERSPLEBEDEB

Learning from an Unimportant Minority: Race Politics Beyond the White/Black Paradigm
J. Sakai • 978-1-894946-60-5
118 pages • $10.00

Race is all around us, as one of the main structures of capitalist society. Yet, how we talk about it and even how we think about it is tightly policed. Everything about race is artificially distorted as a white/Black paradigm. Instead, we need to understand the imposed racial reality from many different angles of radical vision. In this talk given at the 2014 Montreal Anarchist Bookfair, J. Sakai shares experiences from his own life as a revolutionary in the united states, exploring what it means to belong to an "unimportant minority."

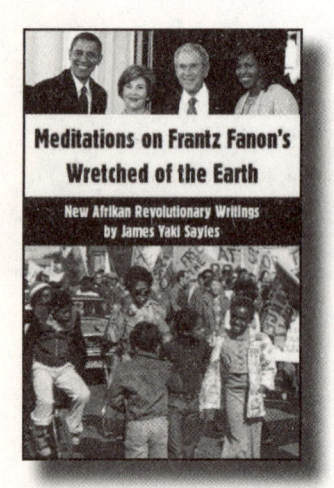

Meditations on Frantz Fanon's Wretched of the Earth: New Afrikan Revolutionary Writings
James Yaki Sayles • 978-1-894946-32-2
399 pages • $20.00

One of those who eagerly picked up Fanon in the '60s, who carried out armed expropriations and violence against white settlers, Sayles reveals how, behind the image of Fanon as race thinker, there is an underlying reality of antiracist communist thought. "This exercise is about more than our desire to read and understand Wretched *(as if it were about some abstract world, and not our own); it's about more than our need to understand (the failures of) the anti-colonial struggles on the African continent. This exercise is also about us, and about some of the things that We need to understand and to change in ourselves and our world." —James Yaki Sayles*

ALSO FROM KERSPLEBEDEB

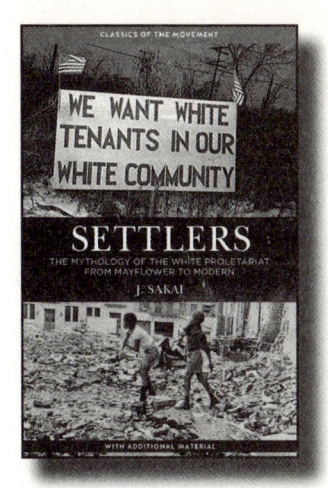

Settlers: The Mythology of the White Proletariat from Mayflower to Modern

J. Sakai • 978-1-62963-037-3
456 pages • $20.00

J. Sakai shows how the United States is a country built on the theft of Indigenous lands and Afrikan labor, on the robbery of the northern third of Mexico, the colonization of Puerto Rico, and the expropriation of the Asian working class, with each of these crimes being accompanied by violence. In fact, America's white citizenry have never supported themselves but have always resorted to exploitation and theft, culminating in acts of genocide to maintain their culture and way of life. This movement classic lays it all out, taking us through this painful but important history.

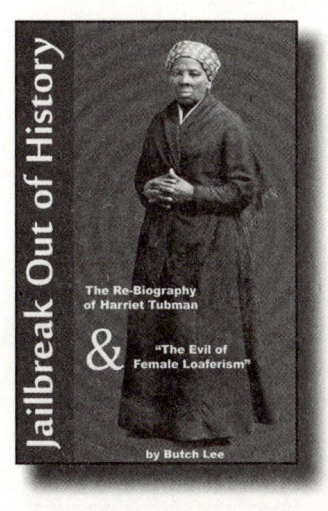

Jailbreak Out of History: the Re-Biography of Harriet Tubman

Butch Lee • 978-1-894946-70-4
169 pages • $14.95

The anticolonial struggles of New Afrikan/Black women were central to the unfolding of 19th century amerika, both during and "after" slavery. The book's title essay, "The Re-Biography of Harriet Tubman," recounts the life and politics of Harriet Tubman, who waged and eventually lead the war against the capitalist slave system. "The Evil of Female Loaferism" details New Afrikan women's class struggles against capitalists North and South.

ALSO FROM KERSPLEBEDEB

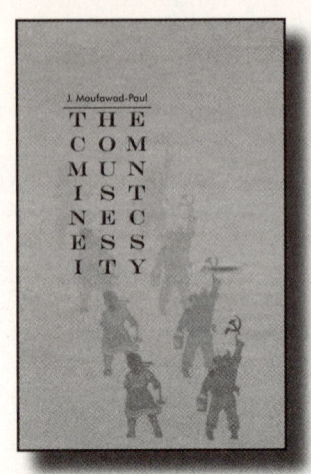

The Communist Necessity

J. Moufawad-Paul • 978-1-894946-58-2
168 pages • $10.00

A polemical interrogation of the practice of "social movementism" that has enjoyed a normative status at the centres of capitalism. Aware of his past affinity with social movementism, and with some apprehension of the problem of communist orthodoxy, the author argues that the recognition of communism's necessity "requires a new return to the revolutionary communist theories and experiences won from history."

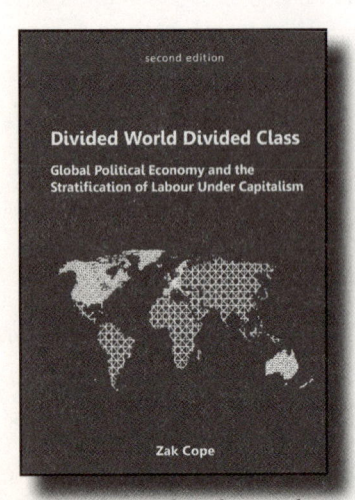

Divided World Divided Class: Global Political Economy and the Stratification of Labour Under Capitalism
SECOND EDITION

Zak Cope • 978-1-894946-68-1
460 pages • $24.95

This book demonstrates not only how redistribution of income derived from superexploitation has allowed for the amelioration of class conflict in the wealthy capitalist countries, it also shows that the exorbitant "super-wage" paid to workers there has meant the disappearance of a domestic vehicle for socialism, an exploited working class. Rather, in its place is a deeply conservative metropolitan workforce committed to maintaining, and even extending, its privileged position through imperialism. This second edition includes new material such as data on growing inequality between the richest and poorest countries, responses to critiques surrounding the thesis of mass embourgeoisement through imperialism, and more.

Kalikot Book Series

V.I. Lenin famously wrote that, "Without revolutionary theory there can be no revolutionary movement."

However, such a revolutionary theory adept to solving the theoretical problems faced by the contemporary revolutionary left has been largely unforthcoming or unavailable. Additionally, due to a prevalent Eurocentrism in North American and European radical traditions, books by or about Third World revolutionaries and their movements remain often unheeded and dismissed. Ignorance of these movements, their movements, and their organic intellectual production has not been entirely willful as the capacity to translate, publish, and distribute such materials in English has remained limited. Thus, their voices and experiences remain largely unknown to revolutionaries around the world.

Kalikot Book Series aims to fill that gap through translating, compiling and publishing books that have been previously unavailable to North American and European audiences. This book series hopes to publish the work of theoreticians and activists from around the world, not only the Third World, that advocate a wide variety of marginalized revolutionary politics. These are books that seek to serve as interventions into numerous complicated problems faced by the contemporary revolutionary left and to not only educate, but to help forge a revolutionary movement capable of the tasks before it.

email: dhruvj@gmail.com
web: http://kalikotbooks.wordpress.com

KERSPLEBEDEB

Since 1998 Kersplebedeb has been an important source of radical literature and agit prop materials.

The project has a non-exclusive focus on anti-patriarchal and anti-imperialist politics, framed within an anticapitalist perspective. A special priority is given to writings regarding armed struggle in the metropole, and the continuing struggles of political prisoners and prisoners of war.

The Kersplebedeb website presents historical and contemporary writings by revolutionary thinkers from the anarchist and communist traditions.

Kersplebedeb can be contacted at:

> Kersplebedeb
> CP 63560
> CCCP Van Horne
> Montreal, Quebec
> Canada
> H3W 3H8
>
> email: info@kersplebedeb.com
> web: www.kersplebedeb.com
> www.leftwingbooks.net

Kersplebedeb